REVOLUTIONARY FORGIVENESS

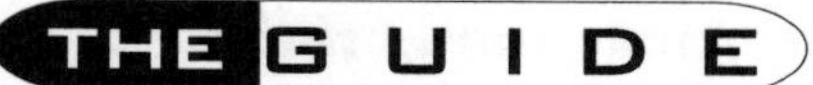

REVOLUTIONARY FORGIVENESS

Developing a forgiving lifestyle

Eric E. Wright

EVANGELICAL PRESS
Faverdale North Industrial Estate, Darlington, DL3 0PH, England

Evangelical Press USA
P. O. Box 84, Auburn, MA 01501, USA

e-mail: sales@evangelicalpress.org
web: http://www.evangelicalpress.org

First published 2002

British Library Cataloguing in Publication Data available

ISBN 0 85234 525 9

Printed and bound in Great Britain by Creative Print and Design Wales, Ebbw Vale, South Wales.

CONTENTS

PREFACE

Why this book? What gift could we give our society that would make the greatest difference to the greatest number of lives? As I think back over my childhood, as I interact with business clients, as I read the newspaper, as I listen to church problems and as I ponder the maturing of my marriage, I have no doubt about the answer: the giving and receiving of forgiveness.

Almost every day some item in a newspaper, some TV segment, some situation in the community or the plot of some novel heralds the importance of forgiveness. My interest in the subject has steadily increased through sixteen years of missionary service and sixteen years of pastoral involvement. Wherever I have served as pastor, I have found others struggling with bitterness and fractured relationships. I have struggled myself!

Learning to give and receive forgiveness is an essential element of Christian living. Without it our relationships become brittle and tattered — or nonexistent. Forgiveness stifles the shrill voice of conflict, heals hurts and renews broken relationships.

This does not mean that forgiveness is popular. C. S. Lewis has commented that forgiveness is the only Christian virtue more unpopular than chastity. Why? Because it is so unnatural. Our fallen psyches seem to derive a perverse sense of satisfaction from fanning sparks of anger into a steady flame of resentment that feeds the engines of revenge and retaliation. Forgiveness quenches the fire. Bitterness fizzles. Hatred dies.

This book grew out of a series of newspaper columns I wrote for the *Christian Week* and *Evangelical Times*. Letters received indicated appreciation for the practical, yet challenging, nature of the columns. Since many issues had to be dealt with briefly and some issues ignored altogether, a book seemed appropriate. Wherever I have mentioned this project, response has been uniformly positive.

Why another book on forgiveness? Until a decade or so ago, most books on forgiveness focused on God forgiving sinners. Since then a number of good books have been written on how we ought to forgive one another. Many of them contain helpful insights. Some, however, are rooted too shallowly in Scripture and too deeply in psychology. Some are too experiential for my taste. Others are very scriptural, but have few practical illustrations.

In spite of all that has been written on the subject, some principles seem to have been overlooked. I did not find any writer distinguishing between forbearance and forgiveness — the patience we need when dealing with human foibles and the forgiveness we need in dealing with human sin. Nor did I discover any book that clarified the cycle of alienation that feeds unforgiveness. Most surprising, the difference between how individual Christians and Christian congregations should deal with forgiveness was not defined.

Nevertheless, I discovered much helpful material in the literature on this subject. I have quoted extensively. My quotations, however, do not mean that I agree with everything written by the authors quoted.

I have added several study questions at the end of every chapter. These are, of course, optional — meant for the person who wants to dig deeper into the subject. They can be used by individuals or become the basis for discussion in a Sunday school class or small group. While the questions are based on the material in the chapter they follow, they are meant to stimulate further study of the biblical text and application of the principles in real life.

I want to especially thank all those who have encouraged me with their feedback. Mary Helen, as always, has been with me all the way. Her keen editorial eye and practical nature has been invaluable.

After you have read this volume, I would encourage you to write to me with comments, corrections and suggestions.

Eric E. Wright
Garden Hill, Ontario
November 2002

HOW TO USE *THE GUIDE*

Revolutionary forgiveness is the fifth book in a new series called *The Guide*. This series will cover books of the Bible on an individual basis, such as *Colossians and Philemon*, and relevant topics such as *Christian comfort* and this work on forgiveness. The series aim is to communicate the Christian faith in a straightforward and readable way.

Each book in *The Guide* will cover a book of the Bible or topic in some detail, but will be contained in relatively short and concise chapters. There will be questions at the end of each chapter for personal study or group discussion, to help you to study the Word of God more deeply.

An innovative and exciting feature of *The Guide* is that it is linked to its own web site. As well as being encouraged to search God's Word for yourself, you are invited to ask questions related to the book on the web site, where you will not only be able to have your own questions answered, but also be able to see a selection of answers that have been given to other readers. The web site can be found at www.evangelicalpress.org/TheGuide. Once you are on the site you just need to click on the 'select' button at the top of the page, according to the book on which you wish to post a question. Your question will then be answered either by Michael Bentley, the web site co-ordinator and author of *Colossians and Philemon*, or others who have been selected because of their experience, their understanding of the Word of God and their dedication to working for the glory of the Lord.

Other books published in the series are *The Bible book by book*, *Colossians and Philemon*, *Ecclesiastes* and *Esther*, and many more will follow. It is the publisher's hope that you will be stirred to think more deeply about the Christian faith, and will be helped and encouraged in living out your Christian life, through the study of God's Word, in the difficult and demanding days in which we live.

CHAPTER ONE

FORGIVENESS — RARE BUT REVOLUTIONARY

LOOK IT UP

'Blessed is he whose transgressions are forgiven,whose sins are covered' (Psalm 32:1).

INTRODUCTION

This book is about forgiveness: offering forgiveness; receiving forgiveness; rejoicing in forgiveness; living free of bitterness and smouldering anger. It is about receiving God's mercy and taking up his challenge to embrace a lifestyle of revolutionary forgiveness. It is about following Jesus, the model forgiver. Simple, really. Well ... maybe not so simple, but eminently possible through the transforming power of the Holy Spirit!

Our granddaughter Kassandra grimaced. Tears began to well up in her eyes. The problem? Asking for forgiveness. She had just hit one of her sisters and her mother was urging her: 'All I want you to do is tell Adrianna you're sorry.' From across the room I could see resistance stiffening her body. Kassandra used every weapon in her four-year-old arsenal in an attempt to avoid saying those two little words.

'Kassandra, you're not alone with that problem,' I thought, as I remembered how difficult I had found apologizing to my wife, Mary Helen, a few days previously.

Asking forgiveness should not be a major problem, just a few simple words: 'I'm sorry,' or, 'I shouldn't have acted that way. Please forgive me.' A kiss and a hug, and suddenly the gathering gloom would flee before the reflected light of the Great Forgiver — the Sun of Righteousness who loves to shine his light into our dark world.

And yet, from the cradle to the grave, bitterness darkens so many of our lives. We can understand why a child might find saying 'I'm sorry' difficult, but it is much harder to understand why we adults take such an irrational approach to grievances.

The theme runs like a dark thread through many award-winning novels. In his book *What's So Amazing About Grace*? Philip Yancey gives several examples.[1] Garcia Márquez's book, *Love in the Time of Cholera*, portrays a marriage that disintegrates over the failure of the wife to replace soap in the bathroom. The husband exaggerated the problem. The wife refused to admit that she forgot. Since neither would ask forgiveness they slept in separate rooms for seven months and ate in silence.

In *The Knot of Vipers* by François Mauriac, a husband sleeps down the hall from his wife for thirty years. The cause was a rift over whether the husband had expressed enough concern for their sick daughter.

In *The Liar's Club*, her memoir of a dysfunctional family, Mary Karr tells of an uncle who did not speak with his wife for forty years after a fight over how much she spent on sugar. 'One day he took out a lumber saw and sawed their house exactly in half. He nailed up planks to cover the raw sides and moved one of the two halves behind a copse of scruffy pine trees on the same acre of ground… They lived out the rest of their days in separate half-houses.'[2]

Stories like these reflect the tip of an iceberg of alienation that plagues humanity around the globe. Its frigid presence has led to blighted families and lonely people, guilt-ridden lives and chaotic courts, wealthy lawyers and rapidly escalating divorce rates; with a subsequent increase in single-parent families, fractured partnerships, grudges, sniping among office associates, name-calling, feuds, and vendettas.

Far from being restricted to one-on-one relationships, bitterness has also blighted ethnic and political relations on every continent in every period of history, with Jewish-Palestinian enmity; tensions in Northern Ireland; English-French ill will in Canada; black-white rancour; and Tutsi-Hutu hatred in Africa.

Resentment and bitterness, with an attendant refusal to apologize or seek reconciliation between parties, have written most of human history. In some circles, offering an apology is viewed as a weakness. Revenge is an honourable duty in many cultures. Consider several examples from both current affairs and more distant history.

- Anti-Semitism has stained much of history with blood. Medieval Christians, refusing to acknowledge the role of all humanity in the death of Christ, blamed the Jewish people. Many of our Jewish friends accurately point to this erroneous belief as the rationale behind the actions of 'Christian nations' in the Crusades and during the Spanish Inquisition. They also point to the church's widespread failure to oppose Hitler's holocaust.
- Many modern Muslims continue to hold all Christians accountable for the atrocities of the Crusades in the eleventh and twelfth centuries.
- Perversely, many politicians have been admired for their refusal to admit culpability. The tough, in-your-face arrogance of Pierre Trudeau, a former prime minister of Canada who refused to apologize when he was shown to be wrong, seemed to endear him to the populace.
- It could be argued persuasively that the gargantuan size of the civil justice system with all its courts, judges and lawyers indicates a propensity to litigate rather than resolve conflicts. The huge backlog of cases in many western courts points to an unhealthy growth in our society's desire to settle for nothing less than a pound of flesh from one's opponent — to squabble, sue and retaliate whatever the cost.
- In recent years, nothing epitomizes the thirst for revenge more than the terrorist attack on the United States on September 11, 2001. But revenge for what? American power? Support of Israel? Stationing troops on Saudi soil? This act of revenge inflicted

TO SUMMARIZE

horrific suffering on thousands of innocent people from over sixty countries who happened to be working in or visiting the World Trade Centre at the time of the attack.

TO SUMMARIZE

Resistance to forgiveness is found throughout our society, from the politician to the most ordinary person. It lives under every guise, and is characterized by a feeling on the part of the people involved that it is in some way justified.

Although negative examples seem much more prevalent, occasionally the power of forgiveness has been recognized:

- Once while attending services in the cathedral at Frankfort, Otto the Great encountered an emaciated man dressed in sackcloth who fell at his feet and pleaded for mercy. Upon recognizing the penitent as the brother who had years before treated him very badly, he pushed him away with his foot. Just then he heard the minister reading from Matthew 18 about forgiving a brother seventy times seven. Stricken, he returned to where his brother lay sobbing, raised him to his feet, and planted a kiss of pardon on his brow. From that day the brother became his most trusted helper.

- In a review of the Watergate scandal that propelled Richard Nixon from office as the U.S. president, CBS commentator Dan Rather ventured that if Nixon had admitted wrongdoing and asked the American people for forgiveness, he would have survived.[3] The continued high ranking of Bill Clinton in the polls following the public confession of fault in his affair with Monica Lewinsky gives some credence to this view.
- In a recent programme on palliative care for the terminally ill it was pointed out that the dying need to say, 'I forgive you', or 'Please forgive me,' before they die. Those who approach death without seeking reconciliation with estranged family members suffer much more than those who are at peace with their relatives.

Failure to give and receive forgiveness continues to be, as it has been since the dawn of human history, an enormous social problem with the direst of consequences. So important is the matter of forgiveness that Morton Weinfeld, Director of McGill University's Ethnic Studies Program, has written that 'Societies can be judged best not by their sins but by the nature of their atonement or redress... Our debt to aboriginal Canadians is greatest, and it remains unpaid. We are diminished as a result.'[4] Note his, perhaps unconscious, use of a religious term — atonement, a central biblical concept.

ILLUSTRATION

We'll deal with how God takes the initiative to provide atonement for our sins in chapter three. Without atonement justice cannot be redressed and guilt cannot be relieved.

These few examples portray our universal need to give and receive forgiveness. They also demonstrate the revolutionary change forgiveness can inject into hostile situations. Surely, then, those of us who have been forgiven by God should be the first to offer and receive forgiveness. But no! Unfortunately, bitterness is all too common in our churches.

- The chairman of the church's nomination committee is informed: 'Don't put them on the same committee. Their families have never got along since their fathers disagreed on the building project in '65.'
- When the church board rejects a favourite project, a deaconess stops going to church and takes up golf.
- A middle-aged woman approaches her pastor concerning reconciliation with her divorced husband. She claims that they are both Christians, but that harsh words after a quarrel led to twenty-five years of alienation. Their family has suffered terribly. Each has been too proud to ask the other for forgiveness. But now, with her husband in hospital, she wants to remarry.
- Ever since his clash with a pastor, Jim Jenkins (not his real name) rebuffs any attempt to

involve him in church life. The pastor admitted his fault and was reconciled to Jim before moving on to another congregation. Jenkins, however, refuses to forgive the elders who failed to support him at that time.

Uncommon? Unfortunately not. During my years as a pastor one of my first tasks in a new church has often been to deal with any real or perceived bitterness that lingers as a legacy from the past.

Not that I'm eager to point the finger at others. After forty-six years of following Christ, I still struggle to say, 'I'm sorry, forgive me.'

THINK ABOUT IT

Ernest Hemingway was brought up in a family whose grandparents attended evangelical Wheaton College. His devout parents, however, hated his libertine lifestyle so much that 'after a time his mother refused to allow him in her presence'. Instead of radiating grace and forgiveness, his mother thought of creative ways to burden him down with feelings of guilt. Hemingway never got over his enmity towards her and her Saviour.

Quoted in Yancey, *What's So Amazing About Grace*? p. 38.

Are there examples from current events or from your own experience that affect your witness and life as a Christian?

Why is the problem so prevalent among Christians when our eternal destiny is secured through the forgiving grace of God? We all know the parable of the servant who was forgiven and his debt of millions of pounds cancelled, but who then rejected an appeal from a fellow servant to forgive an insignificant debt (Matthew 18:21-35). Such conduct in Christians creates a jarring dissonance when laid alongside the cry of Jesus from the cross: 'Father forgive them for they know not what they do.'

Every time we pray in harmony with Jesus' model prayer we ask the Father to 'Forgive us our debts, as we also have forgiven our debtors... For if you forgive men when they sin against you, your heavenly Father will also forgive you. But if you do not forgive men their sins, your Father will not forgive your sins' (Matthew 6:12, 14-15).

An unforgiving lifestyle calls into question our identity as children of God. After all, as peach trees do not produce lemons, neither does the Great Forgiver produce bitter children.

In one sense forgiveness should be a very simple practice to embrace. And yet it is theologically profound, intertwined as it is with biblical concepts such as atonement, reconciliation, pardon, remission, justification and propitiation. But that is as it should be. Theology and practice are two sides of the

Christian coin. Theology without application is hypocrisy and practice that is not based on theology is dangerous.

Forgiveness is one of the most practical and down-to-earth aspects of the Christian faith. It exemplifies grace and mercy. It demonstrates what love is all about. It is restorative, constructive, encouraging and transforming. Forgiveness is a beautiful thing!

What would happen to society if everyone could begin each day with a slate wiped free of grievances, bitterness, anger, failure and sin? If each sunrise saw us waking to a day purified from all of the fallout of our relational wars? What would happen in our churches? What would happen in the workplace? What would happen among nations? What would happen in our families?

Hope, however, is tempered by reality. In spite of the fact that forgiveness knits together the fraying strands of torn relationships like nothing else, there is something in human nature that rises up in resistance to its application. Forgiveness is an incendiary concept to all who are self-righteous, to all who poison their lives with bitterness, to all who give resentment the soil in which to grow. It is as if there is an 'unforgiveness' gene spliced into our DNA. We seem to view saying 'I'm sorry' as if it were a fundamental attack on our ego. We worry that succumbing to its lure will weaken fundamentally the defences we have spent years building up. We act as if admission that we were wrong would explode the castle of self-esteem we have laboured so hard to build. And so families continue to break up, friendships crash, churches split and nations divide and go to war.

Yet when forgiveness is offered, revolutionary things occur. Henry Van Dyke tells of a young labourer who lost a valuable tool only to recognize it later in the toolkit of a fellow employee. Realizing that he was the only Christian in the small factory, the young labourer felt an obligation to live what he believed. Consequently, he went to the offender and said, 'I see you have one of my tools, but you may keep it if you need it.' Going back to work he put the incident out of his mind. During the next three weeks, however, the thief tried three times to give back the value of the tool. Soon the thief and the young labourer became fast friends because, as the thief explained: 'I couldn't stand being forgiven.' Van Dyke comments that 'Loving forgiveness is probably the most powerful tool the Christian has in his kit of virtues'.[5]

Whether exercised in a western factory or in an African village, Christian forgiveness is a revolutionary force. The story is told of the wife of a Zulu chief who was converted after attending a gospel meeting. Upon hearing of her conversion, her husband forbade her to ever attend such a service again. However, the power of the gospel had been so magnetic that she felt compelled to hear more. Discovering her absence, the chief met her on the way back from the meeting and beat her so savagely that he left her for dead. Later his curiosity moved him to go back and look for her. After a considerable search, he found her lying under a bush. '"And what can your Jesus Christ do for you now?" he hissed with hatred in his glance. She opened her eyes, and, looking at him with a sweetness he had never seen before, said gently, "He helps me to forgive you!"'[6]

The astonishing response of this Zulu woman demonstrates the revolutionary nature of forgiveness — it also raises many questions. Where did she get the strength to reject anger and reply lovingly? How could she forgive him until he confessed his abusive behaviour? After all, he was not repentant. Questions such as these, and many more, will be discussed in Part Two: 'Practical questions about forgiveness'. But first we need to draw back the curtain on some unpleasant facts about human nature and some astonishing facts about God's grace.

QUESTIONS FOR DISCUSSION

1. *Give examples, not mentioned in the chapter, of forgiveness — or its lack — from current events, the media or from your own experience.*

2. *Forgiveness is an important theme throughout the Bible. Examine the following passages and list the principles*

DISCUSS IT

about forgiveness that you discover there: Genesis 50:15-21; Leviticus 6:1-7; 2 Chronicles 6:24-25; Psalm 32:1-5; Matthew 18:21-22; Ephesians 4:29-32; 1 John 1:8-10.

3. *What does the parable found in Matthew 18:23-35 tell us about forgiveness and human nature?*

Part One

CREATING A CLIMATE OF FORGIVENESS

CHAPTER TWO

GAINING A PERSONAL PERSPECTIVE

LOOK IT UP

BIBLE REFERENCE

'Do nothing out of selfish ambition or vain conceit, but in humility consider others better than yourselves' (Philippians 2:3).

INTRODUCTION

To a greater or lesser degree, we have all experienced emotions that run the gamut from annoyance through righteous indignation to unreasonable anger that makes us grit our teeth in frustration. We provoke others and are provoked scores of times each day. Perhaps we cannot resist reminding our wife that her 'health' (meaning her weight) does not permit her that piece of lemon cream pie. Or she cannot resist commenting before friends that in spite of high cholesterol, we continue to eat fish and chips. We blow our horn and shake our fist at a car that cuts in on us in traffic. At a sales meeting, our manager reports again that we have not met our sales target during the past three months. A brother taunts his sister about her pimples.

Anger is endemic in the human race. Even while we condemn anger in others we justify it in ourselves. In the situations above, the unconscious reasons we give ourselves might include: 'I'm looking out for my wife's health — besides, she always makes jibes about my middle-aged spread.' 'He's going to have a stroke if he doesn't stop eating those greasy fries.' 'That driver could cause an accident!' 'My sister keeps calling me a geek.'

Larry Crabb writes: 'With frightening ease, we assume that our anger is justified. Without thinking it through, we see our anger as reasonable, natural, warranted by what's happened, and therefore quite acceptable … we automatically justify it … by interpreting other people's actions as adequate cause.' He goes on to point out, however, that 'Anger tells us something about ourselves that deserves attention, something that will need to be exposed and changed before we can move along the path to mature love.'[1]

Yes, anger tells us something about ourselves. In this, as in redemption itself, it is when we 'know the truth' that 'the truth will set [us] free' to walk the paths of peace: truth about ourselves; truth about others; truth about God; truth about Christ. In the chapters ahead we'll discuss how truth about the Father and the Son prepares us to forgive. But first we need to face the truth about the fallen humanity we share with all the sons and daughters of Adam. Why? Because our failure to give and receive forgiveness can usually be traced to blindness about our own foibles, failures and, most important, our personal sinfulness. We almost invariably view ourselves as the innocent victims of others' carelessness or malice. We need a more accurate perspective.

After a night of prayer on the Mount of Olives, Jesus appeared in the temple courts. Immediately, people gathered around him and he sat down to teach. Seeing an opportunity to discredit him, 'the teachers of the law and the Pharisees brought in a woman caught in adultery' (John 8:3).

Imagine the state of this woman, humiliated and facing death at the hands of a blood-thirsty mob carrying rocks to stone her. Caught in the very act of adultery and dragged to the temple, her clothing torn, hair in disarray, face contorted with anguish and fear, tears streaming down her face, she wanted to curl up on the pavement with her hands over her face to escape the venom of her tormentors.

Like vultures with two victims in view — Jesus and the woman — her accusers forced her to her feet. Then they demanded that Jesus either concur with their sentence of immediate justice or prove himself guilty of despising the law. 'Teacher, this woman was caught in the act of adultery. In the law Moses commanded us to stone such women. Now what do you say?' (John 8:4-5).

Instead of directly answering their question, Jesus silently wrote on the ground with his finger. When they continued to badger him, he straightened up, looked them in the eye and said, 'If any one of you is without sin, let him be the first to throw a stone at her' (John 8:7). I imagine that the oldest Pharisee left first with a pinched look on his face, followed by a respected teacher. As conviction for their own sins punctured their self-righteousness, the rest of her accusers slunk away.

Straightening up again, Jesus looked around and saw only the woman still standing there, a dazed look on her face. 'Woman, where are they? Has no one condemned you?' he asked.

'No one, sir,' she replied. Perhaps she cringed, wondering if this strange man who wrote in the dust would now take up stones to kill her. After all, she could not deny her guilt.

Instead she heard words that would re-echo along the corridors of her mind through all the years ahead. 'Then neither do I condemn you. Go now and leave your life of sin.'

THINK ABOUT IT

'The plain truth is that a right knowledge of sin lies at the root of all saving Christianity… Dim or indistinct views of sin are the origin of most of the errors, heresies, and false doctrines of the present day. If a man does not realize the dangerous nature of his soul's disease, you cannot wonder if he is content with false or imperfect remedies.'

J.C. Ryle, *Holiness*, James Clarke Co., reprint 1956, p. 1.

Jesus did not overlook the sordid facts of this woman's licentious lifestyle, but he did offer mercy. Imagine the conviction his merciful words aroused within her soul. No further blows to flog her lacerated conscience; no words of condemnation. Forgiveness, cleansing and a call to genuine repentance offered hope

EXPLANATION

that life could begin anew. Imagine the revulsion she began to feel towards her old life, the longing Jesus' gentle treatment stirred within her for a life free from degradation.

If Jesus, the Judge of all the earth, could treat an undisputed sinner with such mercy, surely we need to examine carefully our own perspective on one another's sins. We dare not view others from a viewpoint of superiority, while harbouring self-righteousness or hypocrisy, prejudice or condemnation. The flag of mercy must fly over all our relationships. That will only be possible if the Holy Spirit leads us to acquire at least some understanding of our own depravity.

Where self-understanding (humility) is missing, pride and hypocrisy hold sway. Pride is an inflated view of oneself. It is arrogance, conceit or haughtiness arising from an exaggerated self-esteem. While most of us abhor conceit in others, we often fail to recognize its presence in our own breast. 'The pride of life' is one of the three windows through which the tempter entices us (see 1 John 2:15-17). To expose our susceptibility to this many tentacled monster called pride, we need to consider Jesus' views on the subject.

Jesus reserved his sternest rebukes for the religious leaders of his day because of their pride and hypocrisy. In Matthew 23 he pronounces seven woes on 'the teachers of the law and the Pharisees' who:

- Do not practise what they preach;
- Practise their religion to be honoured by others;
- Justify themselves while they condemn others;
- Treat others harshly while they treat themselves lightly;
- Focus on externals while neglecting justice, mercy and faithfulness;
- Give an appearance of holiness while inside they are full of evil;
- Profess innocence while they act maliciously.

Jesus recognized that this self-righteous attitude was so deliberate and malignant that he cried out: 'You snakes! You brood of vipers! How will you escape being condemned to hell?' (Matthew 23:33). Although their conduct was transparently hypocritical to others, they remained so blind to their own culpability that they felt justified in plotting Jesus' death. Self-righteousness is a ruinous form of self-deception. No wonder Jesus sought to break through their blindness by the force of harsh words designed to cast light on their true condition.

Jesus illustrated their blindness in a parable designed to expose 'some who were confident of their own righteousness and looked down on everybody else' (Luke 18:9).

This was the story of two men who went up into the temple to pray. As one of them, a Pharisee, came in, he looked around to make sure others saw his display of piety. Some distance away, he spied a tax collector, reviled by society as a greedy thief and traitor. As the

EXPLANATION

Pharisee turned to pray, instead of glorifying God, he reminded God of the dimensions of his righteousness. 'God, I thank you that I am not like other men — robbers, evildoers, adulterers — or even like this tax collector. I fast twice a week and give a tenth of all I get' (Luke 18:11-12).

By contrast the other man, the tax collector, could not lift up his face towards heaven but instead 'beat his breast and said, "God, have mercy on me, a sinner"' (18:13).

Jesus explains that the lesson of the parable can be summarized by saying that the tax collector 'rather than the other, went home justified before God. For everyone who exalts himself will be humbled, and he who humbles himself will be exalted.'

The Pharisee exalted himself, justified himself, because he had no understanding of his own sinfulness. He was blind — and unmerciful. On the other hand, the tax collector knew he was a sinner. He confessed his sins and cried out for mercy. Self-knowledge of this kind not only leads to conviction, confession and repentance but also prepares us to offer forgiveness to others.

You may say, 'I know I'm not perfect — but I'm not a Pharisee nor a greedy tax collector.' Actually, whatever we think or feel about ourselves is highly suspect. Jeremiah, commenting on the infinite capacity of the human heart to deceive itself, wrote: 'The heart is deceitful above all things and beyond cure. Who can understand it?' (Jeremiah 17:9). As fallen children of Adam and Eve we are unconsciously self-deceptive. In verse 10, Jeremiah points out that God alone understands the convolutions of the human heart.

We seldom recognize the extent of our corruption. With an expectant crunch, I bit into a perfectly formed apple only to grimace at the taste. Half an inch below the surface the apple was rotten to the core. Like that apple we must look beneath the surface if we would discover the source of human degradation. The religious leaders of Jesus' day took great pains to appear godly. They emphasized ceremonial cleanliness through rituals and traditions: what they wore; how they cut their hair; where they prayed; how they washed; and what they ate. Jesus forced them to look behind their surface actions to the seat of their hypocrisy. 'Out of the heart come evil thoughts, murder, adultery, sexual immorality, theft, false testimony, slander. These are what make a man "unclean"' (Matthew 15:19-20). Every single human being comes into this world with a heart not only fatally infected by evil but also blinded by self-deception.

TO SUMMARIZE

We have seen that hypocrisy often leads to pride, and pride to a lack of forgiveness. We recognize problems in others, but somehow fail to see ourselves as others see us — frequently in need of forgiveness and condemned by our own criticism of others!

EXPLANATION

Unfortunately, few people today accept this dire diagnosis. We look around and we see nice people. They donate to food banks; help build houses for the poor; volunteer in hospitals; are careful to attend church. But lest we harbour doubts about the pervasive depravity of our personalities Paul lays the cards on the table.

'You, therefore, have no excuse, you who pass judgement on someone else, for at whatever point you judge the other, you are condemning yourself, because you who pass judgement do the same things... There is no one righteous, not even one; there is no one who understands, no one who seeks God. All have turned away... There is no one who does good ... for all have sinned and fall short of the glory of God' (Romans 2:1; 3:11-12, 23).

'Wait!' you say. 'I'm not that bad.' True, externally most of us seem to be quite good neighbours, citizens or parents. However, below the surface a host of feelings and desires, combined with selfish and proud motives, agitate the surface of our hearts. Have we read the Sermon on the Mount lately? This is what Jesus says: 'You have heard that it was said to the people long ago, "Do not murder, and anyone who murders will be subject to judgement." But I tell you that anyone who is angry with his brother will be subject to the judgement... But anyone who says, "You fool!" will be in danger of the fire of hell' (Matthew 5:21-22). Hidden anger! Contempt!

Angry speech! Jesus goes on to condemn any form of hidden lust or lack of love.

At this point you may reply: 'What you say may be true of non-Christians. But I am a Christian. I have been saved, forgiven, justified. I have a new heart. I have been welcomed into God's family.'

Wonderful! However, even though saved, believers still grapple with their old natures. Sanctification is a process whereby, through the Spirit, we put to death that old nature and its propensity to sin and self-deception. The old nature is not eradicated until God calls us home to heaven.

Sin is a congenital heart defect that we hide even from ourselves through unconscious self-conceit. Our capacity for self-deception is illustrated by King David. Not content to commit adultery with Bathsheba, he arranged for the death of her husband. And yet apparently he continued to govern as king without feeling any remorse. You may remember that it took the confrontation of Nathan the prophet to break through his self-righteousness. Nathan came to him with the story of a rich man entertaining a traveller. Instead of selecting a lamb from his own extensive flock, he took the beloved lamb of a poor man to serve to his guests. When David reacted with self-righteous anger, Nathan cried, 'You are the man!' (2 Samuel 12:7). Deeply convicted, David confessed his sin.

David is an authentic biblical hero, authentic because the Bible shows his flaws. Heroes without flaws may exist in fantasy literature, but neither in real life nor the Bible. The hymn writer captures the realistic attitude we should have towards our endemic sinfulness: 'Prone to wander, Lord I feel it, prone to leave the God I love.'[2] In Romans 7 Paul cried out, as we all should, 'I know that nothing good lives in me, that is, in my sinful nature. For I have the desire to do what is good, but I cannot carry it out' (v. 18). This must be our attitude as we approach the subject of forgiveness. When we look at others who show more external evidences of bondage to sin than we who are trying to deal with our failings in this respect, we should remind ourselves: 'I would be the same or worse, but for the grace of God.'

Larry Crabb rightly comments: 'The gospel cannot be enjoyed until all excuses for sin are removed.'[3]

THINK ABOUT IT

THINK ABOUT IT

Unrealistic biographies

Steve Brown writes: 'My friend, Fred Smith, says that one shouldn't pick a hero until he or she is dead. That's wise. Once people are dead, what they did or didn't do is settled. If you pick anybody alive, the story isn't over yet and you might get an unpleasant surprise… But, frankly, it's dangerous to have a hero who is dead too. I've given up reading "puff" [fanciful, overly flattering] biographies of "famous" Christians. When I've taken the time to do the research, I've found out that those kinds of biographies

> have done Christians a great disservice. They have created non-existent people whose example doesn't inspire excellence — only despair. In fact, if you are reading a biography of a "great" Christian and that biography doesn't tell you the bad as well as the good about him or her, burn the book. It's a lie and it will only make you feel guilty.'
>
> Steve Brown, 'Who's on the pedestal', *Key Life Network newsletter*, Sept. 2000, p. 4

Understanding our own depravity does not mean we labour under a debilitating cloud of guilt. Fortunately, if we have been regenerated by the Holy Spirit, what Paul says in Romans 5 and 8 is true of us: 'Therefore since we have been justified through faith, we have peace with God through our Lord Jesus Christ... Therefore, there is now no condemnation for those who are in Christ Jesus' (Romans 5:1; 8:1). Instead of suffering beneath a cloud of guilt we can live under the sunshine of God's gracious forgiveness. This balance — a humbling realization of our own proneness to sin existing side-by-side with a joyful awareness of God's grace — can only be produced by the Holy Spirit. Unless God applies redemptive truth at this point, we will vacillate between despair and self-righteousness — and probably, we will be unable to forgive others. But those who rejoice in divine forgiveness are ready to forgive others.

Therefore, the basic attitude we need to adopt when dealing with forgiveness is understanding — an understanding of ourselves — a realization of the potential for evil in our fallen nature. When we begin to understand ourselves, we can begin to understand others.

EXPLANATION

Perfect understanding will always elude us. Our own limited experiences and personal biases are bound to distort our views. In his book *The Freedom of Forgiveness* David Augsburger writes:

> 'To know all is to forgive all' is an ancient proverb housing a half-truth. Understanding underlies forgiveness. But that's only half the truth. Because even perfect understanding of any other person might lead to contempt, not forgiveness. Any human understanding of another human is tainted with our own evil. None of us is good enough to be entrusted with complete knowledge about another.
>
> Our best intentioned attempts 'to understand' that lead us to try deciphering the other person's formula, to attempt unraveling the mysterious tangle of emotions and motivations, can become an exercise in hypocritical superiority. We are tempted to start impugning others' motives, prejudging their attitudes and actions, stereotyping them into some set of cubbyholes that we've constructed... Playing God.
>
> In being understanding we accept the complexity of human motivation, the contradictions in persons that are beyond our explanation... Any offender, whatever the offense, deserves the gift of understanding.[4]

Gaining a personal perspective

Whenever we approach a seemingly unforgiveable person we need to remind ourselves of several realities:

- I am a human being; so is this other person.
- I am fallible; so is this person.
- I am a sinner. This person is a sinner.
- I am a forgiven sinner. The forgiveness I enjoy is based not upon anything in me — it is a gracious gift from a merciful God. This person is either already or potentially a forgiven sinner.
- What I see about his or her sin may be only part of the reality. I am not omniscient.

None of this means that we should minimize or condone sin in others. We are not called to agree with unhealthy, destructive or harmful behaviour. Nor does it mean that we, or our church, will not need to confront believers who go astray. The role of graciously leading a person to confess and repent of their sin will be dealt with in another chapter.

Jesus is our model. His approach to the woman caught in adultery reminds us that we are not to overlook sin. He instructed the woman to repent, 'leave your life of sin'. One of the main lessons of the incident, however, concerns self-righteousness. His challenge to her accusers to take up stones — if they were without sin — shows that humility must replace self-righteousness in all our dealings with others. We also need an understanding of how God deals with sin — the subject of the next chapter.

DISCUSS IT

QUESTIONS FOR DISCUSSION

1. *Read Luke 18:9-14.*
   a. *List what is wrong with the Pharisee's attitude towards himself and others in this passage.*
   b. *List what is right about the tax collector's attitude towards himself and God.*

2. *What we think about ourselves should be based on reality. Using the following verses draw up a list of what is universally true about you and me — whoever we might be: Jeremiah 17:9; Romans 3:10-18, 23; Ephesians 2:1-3.*

3. *Paul, the Apostle, wrote the letter to the Romans on the basis both of the revelation God gave him of the gospel, and his own considerable experience as a Christian missionary.*
   a. *In spite of his maturity what struggle does Paul admit continues to rage within him? (Romans 7:21-25).*
   b. *What keeps Paul from discouragement and despair? (Romans 7:25 - 8:11).*

4. *What guidance do the following verses give about the attitudes we should adopt when we relate to others, attitudes similar to both the tax collector in Luke 18 and Paul in Romans 7: Philippians 2:3-8; Romans 12:3; Ephesians 4:2; James 4:6?*

CHAPTER THREE

GAINING A HEAVENLY PERSPECTIVE

LOOK IT UP

BIBLE REFERENCE

'I, even I, am he who blots out your transgressions, for my own sake, and remembers your sins no more' (Isaiah 43:25).

INTRODUCTION

Biblical forgiveness calls us to walk a tightrope, balancing a commitment to uphold God's standards of justice while maintaining a humble sense of our own sinfulness. Without our reaction to the harmful actions of others being moderated by self-awareness, we will never rise above self-righteous anger. Also, we may never be able to get over the feeling that we, or justice itself, have been violated.

When others harm us through carelessness or sin, we frequently take their actions as a serious affront to our person. If someone suggests forgiving the person or forgetting the slight, we tend to feel, or even say out loud, 'It's just not right.' 'Look what he did!' We feel instinctively that extending forgiveness too easily is 'cheap grace'. Ostracizing the person, or attacking his reputation, or subjecting him or her to a verbal tongue-lashing — or the silent treatment — may give us a sense of satisfaction.

Our sense of outrage may or may not be justified. Human beings, however, tend to be emotional, fickle, vengeful, inconsistent and unpredictable. When these vagaries of feeling are added to an almost universal tendency to misunderstand the real causes of alienation the result is disastrous. No wonder attempts to redress grievances, or deal with crimes, are frequently mishandled. Clearly, we need another perspective than our own — God's. Those who know God realize the wisdom of bringing their case to the Judge of all the earth, whose judgements combine consistency with mercy, omniscience and justice. He alone can right wrongs.

At this point I need to insert a warning, something like the one J. I. Packer appended at the beginning of his book, *Hot Tub Religion*. 'Danger! Theologian at Work.'[1] This chapter is going to be heavier than most! It is going to plunge into theology. Now theology may cause you to break out in a rash, but I urge you to persevere. Theology is really not a bad word. It simply means 'knowledge of God'. And we dare not plunge into the messy business of forgiveness without carefully laying out what God thinks about our sin and how he deals with it.

Let's pursue this doctrinal search under several headings.

God and sin

Since all sins are, fundamentally, disobedience to God, we need to address God first when we have any questions about forgiveness. The Ten Commandments, including the six that define human interaction, 'are the commandments the LORD proclaimed'. We are instructed: 'Be careful to do what the LORD your God has commanded you' (Deuteronomy 5:22, 32). In the Sermon on the Mount, Jesus raises the moral stakes by, for example, warning that 'anyone who is angry with his brother will be subject to judgement' (Matthew 5:22). Failure to treat others, even one's enemies, with love and purity, honesty and faithfulness will result in God calling us to account for our actions before the bar of divine justice (see Matthew 5).

Paul points out that 'the wrath of God is being revealed from heaven against all the godlessness and wickedness of men', including sexual impurity between humans, envy, deceit, murder, strife, malice, gossip, slander, insolence, arrogance, pride, parental disobedience and even passing judgement on someone else (Romans 1:18; 1:26 - 2:1). Attitudes and actions such as these call for 'God's judgement' (Romans 2:2). Why? As John points out: 'Everyone who sins breaks the law; in fact, sin is lawlessness' (1 John 3:4). When we sin, we rebel against God's will, as expressed in the commandments of Christ. Sin is 'any want of conformity unto or transgression of, the law of God'.[2]

No wonder David came to God first for mercy and cleansing. Since he knew God, he realized that 'Against you, you only, have I sinned and done what is evil in your sight' (Psalm 51:4).

Whenever we approach those who need to give or receive forgiveness, we must remember that our own personal hurts are not paramount. Sin is an act of rebellion against almighty God.

God takes the initiative

Fortunately, we also discover that sin not only provokes God to anger, but it also moves him to take the initiative in rescuing us from our sins. Ezekiel reiterates three times that God takes 'no pleasure in the death of the wicked, but rather that they turn from their ways and live' (Ezekiel 33:11). Paul reminds us that 'God demonstrates his own love for us in this: While we were still sinners, Christ died for us' (Romans 5:8). John writes: 'For God so loved the world that he gave his one and only Son, that whoever believes in him shall not perish but have eternal life' (John 3:16).

God has always taken the initiative. When Adam and Eve ate the forbidden fruit, God stepped in to cover their nakedness with skins taken from a blood sacrifice. Years later, he called Abraham into his service. From Abraham's seed he created a nation through whom would come the Messiah. He delivered Israel through Moses. He initiated a system of sacrifices at Sinai whereby the people could approach him. Again and again he disciplined them for their sins in the wilderness — and then forgave them. He raised up, first judges, and then kings, to lead them. He sent his prophets among them. He called them back from captivity. And finally in the fulness of time he sent his only Son to become our Saviour. We would do well to follow God's example and take the initiative when faced with a problem requiring forgiveness.

God's balanced approach

Sin often arouses uncontrolled emotion in those it harms. We are emotional creatures, prone to swing between extremes of rage and unconcern, jealousy and apathy, vindictive bitterness and a morally bankrupt tolerance. God, however, is always balanced. He does not lose his temper nor is he ever morally ambivalent. He does not offer mercy by denying justice or lowering his standards of holiness. He acts consistently with his whole character.

Note how the psalmist describes the balance evident in the godhead. 'Righteousness and justice are the foundation of your throne; love and faithfulness go before you' (Psalm 89:14). Mercy, along with love, faithfulness and grace, are facets of his goodness. Our sins not only provoke God to mercy, they also offend his righteousness and justice. They arouse him to righteous anger. Justice requires that punishment be exacted for sins committed. Without action being taken, sin, which creates moral anarchy, would have consequences beyond our imagination. But how can God be just and yet extend mercy?

TO SUMMARIZE

Emotions often cloud our judgement when we face the need to give or receive forgiveness. To gain a proper perspective we should first of all remind ourselves of God's viewpoint. Sin is first and foremost an offence against God. Amazingly, God has always taken the initiative in dealing with sin. If we follow his lead we will not go wrong. He alone approaches us with a balance of mercy and justice. He alone can deal with the cosmic consequences of sin.

God alone can deal with sin's consequences

The proclamation to Isaiah by the seraphs, 'Holy, holy, holy is the LORD Almighty; the whole earth is full of his glory', came in the context of an awesome vision of God in the temple, 'high and exalted' (Isaiah 6:3, 1). This glimpse of the glory of God moved Isaiah to shudder under the burden of the sins he shared with the nation of Israel. He cried: 'Woe to me! ... I am ruined! For I am a man of unclean lips, and I live among a people of unclean lips' (6:5). Fortunately, a seraph flew to him with a live coal from off the altar and said,

'See, this has touched your lips; your guilt is taken away and your sin atoned for' (6:7). The Bible uses a broad range of amazing words in order to capture the astonishing way God deals with the consequences of sin.

1. *Atonement* describes a provision designed by God to enable mankind to become at-one with him. Sin introduced a horrendous breach in the harmonious fellowship mankind enjoyed with God in the Garden of Eden. The rebellion that produced this breach called for punishment. Since 'the wages of sin is death', the question arises as to how God can possibly forgive our sins without exacting that penalty.

In Isaiah's case, the seraph used a coal from the sacrificial altar to convey the effects of atonement to Isaiah. The altar was part of the gracious sacrificial system instituted by God to provide for man's forgiveness. Substitutionary blood sacrifices became God's way of atoning for sin. The balance between mercy and severity was maintained — the sinner could live, the sacrifice die. The shedding of blood, in the death of the sacrificial animal, maintained a sense of the extreme seriousness of sin.

The animals that died pre-figured Christ, the Lamb of God, who died on the cross as our substitute. Isaiah saw him in a prophetic vision. 'He was pierced for our transgressions, he was crushed for our iniquities; the punishment that brought us peace was upon him, and by his wounds we are healed. We all, like sheep, have gone astray, each of us has turned to his own way; and the LORD has laid on him the iniquity of us all' (Isaiah 53:5-6).

Teaching about the purpose of Christ's death pervades the New Testament. 'God presented him as a sacrifice of atonement, through faith in his blood. He did this to demonstrate his justice, because in his forbearance he had left the sins committed beforehand unpunished — he did it to demonstrate his justice at the present time, so as to be just and the one who justifies those who have faith in Jesus' (Romans 3:25-26). Just and justifier. Judge and Forgiver.

Sin has consequences. The only way to escape those consequences is through believing the gospel. The gospel brings us the good news that Christ atoned for our sins to enable God to give us a gift! 'The gift of God is eternal life through Christ Jesus our Lord' (Romans 6:23). Imagine! Christ voluntarily became our substitutionary sacrifice. 'He himself bore our sins in his body on the tree, so that we might die to sins and live for righteousness; by his wounds you have been healed. For you were like sheep going astray' (1 Peter 2:24-25). In matters pertaining to forgiveness, then, our first recourse must be to Jesus Christ and his gospel. Our banner must be the blood-red banner of the cross.

In a sense, the whole Bible is about God dealing with the consequences of human sin. It is the story of a

EXPLANATION

seeking God who takes the initiative in saving us from sin. The Bible uses a wealth of terminology, besides 'atonement', to define various aspects of his saving work — propitiation, redemption, justification, reconciliation, adoption and sanctification.

2. *Propitiation* describes how the anger our sins provoke in God is appeased or pacified. 'Christ Jesus, whom God hath set forth to be a propitiation through faith in his blood' (Romans 3:24-25, AV). 'Herein is love, not that we loved God, but that he loved us, and sent his Son to be the propitiation for our sins' (1 John 4:10, see also 1 John 2:1-2, AV). In this terminology, Christ appeased the wrath of God.

3. *Redemption* signifies that God has incurred great cost in delivering us from the state of sinful captivity in which we lived. Peter wrote that 'It was not with perishable things such as silver or gold that you were redeemed ... but with the precious blood of Christ, a lamb without blemish or defect' (1 Peter 1:18-19).

4. *Justification* is one of the most transforming terms used by the Bible to describe our forgiveness, from God's perspective. It expresses 'the idea of secure, present, and permanent acceptance in the sight of God. It connotes both

a complete and a permanent state of grace,'[3] based upon faith in the atoning sacrifice of Christ. Once justified, a person has 'peace with God through our Lord Jesus Christ' and exists in a state of 'no condemnation' (Romans 5:1; 8:1).

So comprehensive is justification that our besmirched record is wiped clean. God declares: 'I, even I, am he who blots out your transgressions, for my own sake, and remembers your sins no more' (Isaiah 43:25). Although this cannot mean that God no longer knows about our forgiven sins — after all, he is omniscient — it does mean that they are completely erased from God's attention. Jeremiah declares: 'For I will forgive their wickedness and will remember their sins no more' (Jeremiah 31:34). David rejoiced that 'As far as the east is from the west, so far has he removed our transgressions from us' (Psalm 103:12).

5. *Reconciliation* deals with closing the breach between sinners and God. Peace with God is now possible because our sinful record is wiped clean. We are justified. With the righteous record of Christ credited to our account in place of the sins that separated us from God, the breach created by our rebellion can be bridged. This restoration of fellowship is called 'reconciliation'. Paul writes: 'Since we have now been justified by his blood ... we were reconciled to him through the death of his Son ... we also rejoice in God through our Lord Jesus Christ, through whom we have now received reconciliation' (Romans 5:9-11).

EXPLANATION

6. *Adoption* heralds the result of our reconciliation, our acceptance into the family of God. Instead of remaining enemies of God, who deserve his wrath, God adopts us into his family. As his children, the Holy Spirit helps us to cry 'Abba, Father'. And as reconciled children of God we have been given the 'ministry of reconciliation'. We are to become 'peacemakers' committed to announce the gospel message that 'God was in Christ reconciling the world to himself.' We become ambassadors of reconciliation, committed to restoring alienated men and women to their Edenic relationship with God.

7. *Sanctification* reminds us that God is not finished with sinners when they are adopted into his family. Saved sinners are not perfect saints, but damaged souls for whom God has much work to accomplish before he calls them home to heaven. Justification, redemption, reconciliation and adoption, although they occur in an instant, initiate a sanctifying process that continues throughout the believer's life. Paul, Peter and James describe the process whereby God uses troubles and suffering to transform sinners into the image of Christ. 'Suffering produces perseverance; perseverance, character; and character, hope' (Romans 5:3-4). 'Make every effort to add to your faith goodness; and to goodness, knowledge ... self-control ... perseverance; ... godliness ... brotherly kindness ... love. For if

you possess these qualities in increasing measure, they will keep you from being ineffective and unproductive in your knowledge of our Lord Jesus Christ' (2 Peter 1:5-8; see also James 1:2-4).

TO SUMMARIZE

God deals with sin's consequences through:

Atonement: substitutionary sacrifice — Jesus, the Lamb of God
Propitiation: appeasement of the wrath our guilt provokes
Redemption: freedom from sin's bondage through the payment of a price
Justification: perfect cleansing of the sinner's record through applying the righteousness of Christ to the sinner's account
Reconciliation: restoration of fellowship with God
Adoption: acceptance into God's family
Sanctification: the process of transforming sinners into the likeness of Christ, often involving discipline

Discipline denotes how God trains his children. Since God purposes to sanctify all justified sinners, 'The Lord disciplines those he loves' (Hebrews 12:6). While forgiveness involves the removal of guilt, it does not mean that God immediately wipes out all the consequences of our sins. Adam and Eve were forgiven,

EXPLANATION

and yet — as warned — banished from paradise. Their sins were covered by the animal sacrifice God provided, even as their nakedness was covered by the skins from the sacrifice. The corruption they brought upon their nature, however, was passed on to all their future generations. Israel's sins at the foot of Sinai were forgiven, but they had to suffer the discipline of forty years of wandering in the wilderness. David's sin with Bathsheba was forgiven, but the child conceived died. David's sin of numbering Israel was forgiven, but it brought down a terrible plague on the nation. Hosea took his wife home, but she was to live with him for some time before intimacy was restored.

As we seek to imitate God in matters of forgiveness, we would be wise to note that forgiveness does not mean the erasing of all consequences. Restitution may be involved. Reconciliation may require a lengthy re-building of relationships. A murderer might be forgiven, and yet he would have to suffer the civil punishment for his crime. Concerns such as these will be dealt with in more detail in the chapters that follow.

Learning to forgive as God forgives

How does God deal with professing believers who sin? Consider an example from the life of

David. Against the advice of his closest advisors, and contrary to the will of God, David took a census of Israel's fighting men. Apparently, after a long string of victories David had become rather arrogant. Only after the census was complete did David feel conscience-stricken. God sent the prophet Gad to offer David the choice of three kinds of discipline. David responded: 'I am in deep distress. Let us fall into the hands of the LORD, for his mercy is great; but do not let me fall into the hands of men' (2 Samuel 24:14).

It is always wisest to ask God to deal with sin. The history of Israel is a history of mercy. After Ezra had read the law to the exiles who had returned from captivity, they confessed their sins to God and asked for his mercy. They confessed that 'our forefathers became arrogant and stiff-necked, and did not obey your commands. They refused to listen and failed to remember the miracles you performed among them' (Nehemiah 9:16-17). The exiles pondered their people's cycle of rebellion, the judgement that resulted, their subsequent repentance and God's deliverance — followed, unbelievably, by resurgent evil. In spite of a history tarnished by this repeated cycle of rebellion, the returning captives expressed their hope in God by declaring: 'But you are a forgiving God, gracious and compassionate, slow to anger and abounding in love' (9:17). God is infinitely more merciful than human institutions or individuals.

God used the Old Testament prophet Hosea as an illustration of his forgiving grace. Hosea's wife had abandoned him for a series of lovers. In order to demonstrate his mercy for the spiritual adultery of the nation of Israel, God asked Hosea to do the seemingly impossible. 'Go, show your love to your wife again, though she is loved by another and is an adulteress. Love her as the LORD loves the Israelites, though they turn to other gods' (Hosea 3:1). After a life of debauchery, Hosea's wife was so ruined that she was put up for sale in the slave market. Hosea overcame his anguish and revulsion to buy her back, take her home and love her again.

Through Hosea God demonstrates his own love and illustrates how we ought to deal with one another. Like grace, forgiveness is a gift — never earned, just given.

THINK ABOUT IT

'That our idea of God correspond as nearly as possible to the true being of God is of immense importance to us... We tend by a secret law of the soul to move towards our mental image of God ... I believe there is scarcely an error in doctrine or a failure in applying Christian ethics that cannot be traced finally to imperfect and ignoble thoughts about God.'

A. W. Tozer, *The Knowledge of the Holy*, New York: Harper & Row, 1961, pp. 9-10

As in everything else, we will seriously err if God is not our starting point. We can never counter ignoble thoughts of God if we do not approach him with gospel-eyes. The fact that 'Christ died for *our* sins' (1 Corinthians 15:3) must be ever before us. Our status with God rests on the gospel. That gospel proclaims the remission of our sins. Without it we can know nothing about real forgiveness. The joy in experiencing our own forgiveness, however, provides the impetus to approach others with an eagerness to forgive.

As we approach situations involving forgiveness we would do well to remind ourselves of these truths:

1. All sin is first and foremost against God;
2. God takes the initiative in dealing with sin;
3. God alone approaches sinners with a balance of justice and mercy;
4. God alone can deal with the consequences of sin. The gospel celebrates divine grace. That grace crafted the works of atonement, propitiation, redemption, justification, reconciliation, adoption, sanctification and ongoing discipline.
5. How God forgives must be our example.

Saturating our consciousness with thoughts of God and his grace in Jesus Christ will do more than anything else to protect us from faulty approaches to forgiveness. If God can forgive a murderer and adulterer like David and a prostitute such as Hosea's wife, surely he can even forgive me! And if he can forgive me, then we must be ready to forgive those who sin against us. Those who savour God's grace and mercy become gracious and merciful.

DISCUSS IT

QUESTIONS FOR DISCUSSION

1. *Salvation from sin involves atonement, propitiation, redemption, justification, reconciliation, adoption and sanctification. Read Romans 3:19-26 and 5:1-10 and then answer the following questions. Note that the terms sanctification, propitiation and adoption are not used in the texts.*
   a. *Which doctrinal term can be connected with the following phrases? Explain why: 'declared righteous'; 'a righteousness from God apart from the law'; 'comes through faith'; 'apart from observing the law'.*
   b. *Which doctrinal term is connected with the following words and phrases? Explain why: 'Christ died for us'; 'sacrifice'; 'blood'; 'demonstrate his justice at the present time, so as to be just and the one who justifies'; 'died for the ungodly'.*
   c. *Redemption means 'freedom through the payment of a price'. In the text what words are used to indicate the cost to God and the cost to us?*
   d. *Justification deals with being declared righteous through faith in Christ's atonement. Read Romans 1:18 & 5:1, 9. What theological term, not specifically mentioned here, describes appeasing the wrath our sins arouse in God?*
   e. *What doctrinal term in the passage is used to describe restoration of fellowship with God?*

f. *What term, not used specifically in Romans 5:2-5, describes the process indicated here, a process superintended by the Holy Spirit. Notice the important role suffering and tribulation plays in this process.*

2. *Most people today have drifted so far from biblical norms that they find words such as 'sin', 'transgression' and 'evil' repellant. Where sin is acknowledged, emphasis is mainly laid on how it harms human relationships between, for example, brothers and sisters, husbands and wives. Explain how the following verses correct this imbalance: Luke 15:21 with Deuteronomy 5:22, 32-33; and 1 John 3:4 with verses 22 & 32.*

3. *Using Romans 3:19, 27, explain why an understanding of how God deals with our own personal sin must come before we try to right relationships with others that have been strained by sin.*

4. *According to the following verses, what can we learn from God about how we should approach those who have sinned against us: Romans 5:8; Hosea 3:1?*

5. *Discuss why any approach to forgiveness that fails to take into account what God has done in saving sinners from sin is bound to be defective.*

CHAPTER FOUR

UNEARTHING THE BITTER ROOT THAT POISONS FORGIVENESS

LOOK IT UP

BIBLE REFERENCE

'Get rid of all bitterness, rage and anger, brawling and slander, along with every form of malice. Be kind and compassionate to one another, forgiving each other, just as in Christ God forgave you' (Ephesians 4:31-32).

INTRODUCTION

In spite of our exposure to the grace of our Lord Jesus Christ, many of our relationships are chilled by a permafrost of bitterness. The healing that forgiveness brings cannot melt frozen relationships until this underlying permafrost is breached. Otherwise it will be superficial. We need to explore the substrata of our emotions if we are to create a climate conducive to forgiveness.

Most of us acknowledge willingly that we are human — and to be human is to err. This is impossible to deny! Admitting the prevalence of pious self-righteousness in our own heart is more difficult. Perhaps, however, the Holy Spirit has thrown back the sanctimonious curtain we have woven to hide our own depravity in all its horror. Perhaps we have begun to embrace biblical humility. Hopefully, the Spirit has also led us to the feet of Jesus, our suffering Saviour, to receive the liberating application of his precious blood. We know we are justified, adopted, reconciled. We rejoice in grace.

In this two-fold knowledge (of ourselves and of God) we ought to be ready to embrace all human beings with understanding and love. To forgive and to forget. And yet, something keeps us from it. That mysterious kill-joy is often bitterness.

Robert Enright, president of the International Forgiveness Institute, is at the forefront of a new area of study: research into the effects of forgiveness on interpersonal relationships. In writing about the benefits of forgiveness on society he uncovers the problem. 'It is an obvious fact that we live in a world where violence, hatred, and animosity surround us on all sides… We hear much about the "social" causes of crime — poverty, unemployment, and illiteracy, for example. We sometimes hear about the need for tolerance and co-operation, compassion, and understanding. But almost never do we hear public leaders declaring their belief that forgiveness can bring people together, heal their wounds, and alleviate the bitterness and resentment caused by wrongdoing.'[1]

Feelings of bitterness and resentment have always been part of human experience. Victims of crime feel bitter towards criminals. Those who have suffered accidents feel bitterness towards those whose carelessness caused their pain. Workers bitterly resent the companies that exposed them to hazardous chemicals. Children may grow up to feel bitter towards absent parents. Certainly, the bitterness Jewish people harbour towards the 'Christian nations' for centuries of anti-Semitism is relatively easy to grasp. We can even sympathize with the anger aboriginal peoples in many parts of the world feel towards the people who exploited them. We can empathize with blacks who struggle to forget their history of slavery. And who does not feel a wave of anger towards those who abuse women or children?

We can even relate to the bitterness that suffering people may feel towards God. The Bible, realistic book that it is, prepares us for this. After multiple calamities that included the loss of his children and all his wealth, Job, very honestly, said, 'I will not keep silent; I will speak out in the anguish of my spirit, I will complain in the bitterness of my soul' (Job 7:11). As Job discovered, bitterness towards God is never right. It arises from our ignorance of the multiplicity of divine purposes that intersect at any given point of history.

But what about people who have not been the victims of horrendous events? What about those of us who harbour bitterness that seems to come from nowhere — bitterness that springs from imaginary hurts, misunderstandings, or even small annoyances?

A mother wrote to a newspaper columnist about the tragic alienation ruining her family. Ten years earlier her son had objected to something her daughter did. Since he refused to discuss it with her, she never knew what caused his anger. The mother explained: 'Aside from refusing to speak to her, he avoided family functions to which she had been invited. If she happened to drop in to visit a relative and he was present, he would leave immediately making no effort to mask his reason for the hasty departure. He went so far as to change churches to avoid running into her. Since the estrangement, our family has been unable to get together for birthdays, anniversaries or holidays.'[2]

After eight years, the daughter decided to confront the brother in order to discover the cause of the hatred. But when confronted, 'he flew into a rage, cursed, carried on like a maniac and ran out of the house, slamming the door behind him'.[3]

A year or so later it was discovered that the daughter had a terminal illness. Doctors gave her three months to live. This terrible news fell like a hammer blow on the brother's conscience. He came to her bedside to apologize and ask for her forgiveness. Unfortunately, his sister felt that his apology was nothing more than maudlin emotion precipitated by her sickness. She told him how much his friendship would have meant during the previous ten years but refused to accept his apology. Then she asked him not to stay around while she died.

Too many families can tell stories like the one above. Strangely enough, the most common examples of bitterness are not those represented by victims of murder or accident, slavery or abuse, prejudice or injustice. The bulk of human bitterness and resentment sprouts like toadstools in the context of ordinary human relationships like the one described above. Often the seed is sown by some seemingly inconsequential incident or statement. Or it may be due to the friction generated wherever people live and work in close proximity to each other. Fortunately, the result is seldom this extreme.

THINK ABOUT IT

Strangely enough, the bulk of human bitterness cannot be traced to terrible or dramatic causes. No, most often bitterness grows like toadstools in the context of ordinary human relationships — originating through relatively inconsequential actions or statements.

We may not have harboured resentment as long or felt it as deeply as the brother in the example above. But who among us will refuse to admit that we have nurtured some resentment, at some time in our lives, towards husbands or fathers or sisters or neighbours or church members?

A wife resents her husband who escapes (her word) the home with its three small children to work at a challenging job. 'And then he comes home and collapses in front of the TV and won't even help with the kids or the evening dishes.' In turn, he resents her freedom from the stress and pressure of the dog-eat-dog world in which he labours. 'Why can't she use her time better? Why doesn't she appreciate the stresses I work under? Why hasn't she responded romantically during the last month?'

Husbands and wives have heated arguments. The memory of these exchanges can linger in the psyche where they smoulder. Women can resent other women, and men other men. Leah resented Rebekah; Saul resented David (see Genesis 29-30; 1 Samuel 18-19). A woman in her fifties thinks to herself about a business colleague: 'She's only attractive because she's had cosmetic surgery.' A man in a factory job comments about a childhood friend: 'Sure, he makes much more than me, but his father gave him a head start.'

Parents can even resent their children. Jean Walcott Wilson writes that 'Fear, anger, guilt, shame, anxiety and despair can immobilize parents of a rebellious child. This torrent of negative emotions often triggers hasty reactions.'[4] Some resent children when they begin to display character defects that reflect their own depravity. Resentment often moves us to project our guilt on others.

Children can resent their parents. 'Why didn't Dad come to my game?' 'Mum likes my sister more than me.' 'All Dad had time for was to give me a spanking.'

Siblings resent each other. 'Cain was very angry [at God and at his brother Abel] and his face was downcast' (Genesis 4:5). Joseph's brothers were so resentful of him that they sold him into slavery (Genesis 37:11-27). Jacob and Esau were rivals. We are no different today. Children comment: 'My brother gets all the attention'; 'My parents trust my sister but not me'; 'My sister is a teacher's pet, that's why she gets better marks.'

Anger and resentment flourishes in the business and academic world — of bosses, of colleagues who get promotions, of co-workers who get away with cheating, of other businesses, of men who are paid better, of minorities who are fast-tracked, of successful surgeons, even between researchers. It does not matter how professional or how well trained two antagonists may be. The eight scientists who volunteered for a two-year isolation experiment in the biosphere near Tuscon, Arizona, split into two rival groups. During the final months these two groups did not talk to each other.

We even find its bitter fruit where teamwork would seem vital to survival. After a minor dispute, Frank Reed, a hostage in Lebanon, spent several months refusing to talk to a fellow hostage to whom he was chained.[5]

Many people choose another target for their bitterness. They are angry with God. 'Why am I poor?' 'Why did God allow my daughter to die?' 'Why did God let me get cancer? I've always tried to serve him.' 'I did everything right, and yet God allowed my dishonest competitor to be successful.'

Wherever we live, however young or old we are, we will discover bitterness. Much of it is deeply buried. The book of Proverbs informs us: 'Each heart knows its own bitterness' (14:10). Paul points out that bitterness is endemic among the fallen children of Adam. 'There is no one righteous, not even one … their mouths are full of … bitterness' (Romans 3:10, 14).

Even in forgiven sinners this bitter root struggles to strangle the new principle of love implanted by the Spirit. Otherwise why would Christ exhort his disciples when they pray to be sure to forgive their brothers? And why else would Paul exhort believers in Ephesus to give great care to 'Get rid of all bitterness, rage and anger, brawling and slander, along with every form of malice' (Ephesians 4:31)? Clearly, the temptation for Christians to harbour resentment that may kindle 'rage and anger, brawling and slander, along with every form of malice' is very high.

Indeed, Christians are a special target of the evil one. While I may not agree with everything Neil Anderson writes, on this he is on track. He writes: 'Most of the ground that Satan gains in the lives of Christians is due to unforgiveness. We are warned to forgive others so that Satan cannot take advantage of us.'[6]

Paul was concerned that the man disciplined for immorality in Corinth, as commanded in his first letter, had suffered enough and ought to be forgiven, 'in order that Satan might not outwit us. For we are not unaware of his schemes' (2 Corinthians 2:11). Central among the devil's stratagems is his goal to foster bitterness. To counter his schemes we must identify the problem, confess our sins and then cry out to God to pour his forgiving love into our hearts.

Before we can do that, we have to admit that bitterness and resentment are almost as common in Christian circles as in the world at large. This should not surprise us. Imagine the emotions generated in Paul himself, and those who valued his ministry, by those who criticized publicly his appearance, his delivery and his credentials at Corinth. Imagine the resentment aroused by divisions in Corinth, between those following different teachers; those who took each other

ILLUSTRATION

to court; those involved in, and witness to, the sordid story of immorality between a son and his father's wife; those who abstained from food sacrificed to idols and those who vaunted their freedom; women who dressed in different ways; those who ate and drank at the Lord's Table and those who went home hungry; those who boasted of one gift and those who boasted of another?

Many examples of resentment surface in churches at home and abroad. A pastor who had spent decades serving faithfully, but was never able to save anything after paying his bills, became bitter at the congregations who had paid him so poorly. Imperceptibly his sermon delivery changed from being arresting and encouraging to become harsh and judgemental. His son, seeing how hard his mum and dad scraped and saved to make ends meet, determined never to darken the door of a church again.

The accidental failure of the secretary to put Thomas's name on the list of responsibilities at the annual meeting brought Thomas's simmering anger towards the pastor to the surface. In the meeting he accused the pastor of deliberately trying to shift him to the sidelines.

In 1982 Alice had made a joking remark about Nicole's dress being too short. From that moment on, Nicole never talked to Alice again.

In 1995 Norman was rushed to the hospital with a stroke. The pastor was away on a mission trip to South America. The visitation elder was also away on a business trip. No one from the church visited Norman. Although he has recovered and sits at the back of the church, he scowls every time the pastor preaches. He often comments about the church's ineffective visitation programme.

Janice and Marguerite jointly ran the women's weekly Bible study. Two fruitful years went by. At the beginning of the third year, Janice saw her husband laughing with Marguerite who was younger, slimmer and more vivacious than her. From that point on their joint ministry began to fall apart. Marguerite was puzzled by Janice's belligerent responses to discussions about curriculum, scheduling and refreshments. Janice seemed to disagree with her about everything. Marguerite became frustrated and angry. Janice became moody and distant. Half way through that third year, the women's ministry ground to a halt.

Bitterness even rears its ugly head in mission situations. After half a century of missionary work by ten agencies only a few hundred members of a certain people group have become believers. They are scattered throughout a country that I cannot name without endangering their lives. Recently forty of them gathered in a rare time of fellowship and devising strategies. But on the final night of the conference, before a time of sharing in communion, an altercation between two leading believers over an event that had occurred fifteen years previously threatened the whole event. Fifteen years of resentment burst into flame threatening to incinerate a fragile work in an extremely difficult vineyard! As the service continued three other brothers tried to help them resolve their differences. Fortunately they were successful and the two aggrieved brothers re-entered the meeting arm in arm with 'tears on their cheeks and faces aglow.'[7]

TO SUMMARIZE

The Bible gives us many examples demonstrating that feelings of bitterness and resentment have always been part of human experience. Novels and newspapers reflect this reality. Some bitterness can be traced to horrific causes: terrible accidents, crime, the holocaust, slavery or oppression.

Most bitterness, however, has a much more mundane source. It may be traced to imaginary hurts, slights, misunderstandings, small annoyances, differences of temperament, hurtful words or actions — wherever people congregate.

Bitterness may corrupt relationships between husbands and wives, parents and children, pastors and congregants — between siblings, co-workers, neighbours, scientists and even missionaries.

Satan works without let-up to insinuate bitterness between Christians.

Wherever we meet it, we must slay bitterness and resentment. The writer of Hebrews exhorts us: 'Make every effort to live in peace with all men and to be holy... See to it that no one misses the grace of God and that no bitter root grows up to cause trouble and defile many' (Hebrews 12:14-15). If we do not deal swiftly with deteriorating relationships — whether they be in the home, at work or in the church — bitterness puts down roots that will grow to choke loving conversation.

Dealing with this bitter root requires recognition of its presence. In order to become a peacemaker, as commanded by Christ and his apostles, we have to be realistic about our own propensity to bitterness. Let's face the truth! We are good at harbouring grievances. We are poor at dealing quickly and honestly with our sins and foibles.

But do we want to continue to kill the joy of Christ that is our heritage? Allowing bitterness to find residence within us is like living where the weather is perpetually bad. Every morning we wake up to fog or rain, sleet or hail. The temperature is always cold and the sun never shines. The joy of our salvation freezes beneath the frigid feelings that blow in through a door in our psyche opened whenever certain people appear on our horizon.

Before we can give and receive forgiveness we must deal with those feelings we have towards others. That will involve thawing the permafrost of resentment, bitterness and malice that causes relationships to turn to ice — and confessing them to be what they are, sin. But how can we identify the agents of this chill? How can we counter their baneful influence?

DISCUSS IT

QUESTIONS FOR DISCUSSION

1. *Read Hebrews 12:14-15 where we are challenged to enter into close fellowship with God, an experience described as 'seeing the Lord'. How are peaceable living, holiness and the absence of bitterness, or the opposite, linked to living in close fellowship with God, or missing that fellowship?*

2. *In each of the following passages list the circumstances, and people's reactions to them, that led to a root of bitterness springing up.*
   a. *Genesis 4:1-8*
   b. *1 Samuel 18:5-9*
   c. *Job 7:1-11; 9:14-18 (also Job 10:1; 21:25)*
   d. *Ruth 1:1-5, 19-20*

3. *What different attitudes, as described in 1 Corinthians 13:4-7, could the parties in the passages above have adopted to avoid a root of bitterness springing up?*
   a. *Cain*
   b. *Saul*
   c. *Job*
   d. *Naomi*

4. *Using newspaper stories, TV dramas and — most important — life as you know it, illustrate how common bitterness is in life.*

5. *According to 1 John 1:9 and Ephesians 4:31-32, what should we do if we realize that bitterness is present in our heart?*

CHAPTER FIVE

ISOLATING THE CYCLE OF ALIENATION

LOOK IT UP

BIBLE REFERENCE

'What causes fights and quarrels among you? Don't they come from your desires that battle within you?' (James 4:1). 'But now you must rid yourselves of all such things as these: anger, rage, malice, slander and filthy language from your lips' (Colossians 3:8).

INTRODUCTION

As every best-selling author knows, most people relate to books that sketch the human condition against a backdrop of dark and brooding melancholy. Characters reek of resentment, bitterness and unforgiveness. Threads of revenge are woven through the stories. Here and there a cheerful Anne of Green Gables rises above the gloom. Anne-like characters, however, are few. Why is this so? Happy, loving characters who flit through life forgiving and being forgiven strike most people as imaginary; fictitious; chimeras that exist only in a hopeful author's brain.

Down here on planet earth where we live, forgiveness seems unnatural. W. H. Auden wrote:

> I and the public know
> What all school children learn,
> Those to whom evil is done
> Do evil in return.

Philip Yancey comments: 'Auden, who wrote those lines, understood that the law of nature admits no forgiveness. Do squirrels forgive cats for chasing them up trees or dolphins forgive sharks for eating their playmates? It's a dog-eat-dog world out there, not dog-forgive-dog. As for the human species, our major institutions — financial, political, even athletic — run on the same unrelenting principle... The very taste of forgiveness seems somehow wrong.'[1]

Forgiveness is unnatural because it interrupts a natural process. By natural, I do not mean ideal but, rather, defective and sinful — the natural result of our fallenness. Unless interrupted by a measure of forgiveness, an incident provoking anger may ultimately lead to a settled disposition of malice towards the cause of the incident. I call this 'the alienation process'.

Mankind's fall into sin rendered all relationships subject to fracture. In Romans 3 Paul points out that one of the universal characteristics sinners demonstrate is an inability to live at peace with others. 'The way of peace they do not know' (v. 17).

Most importantly, sin alienated us from God. 'Your iniquities have separated you from your God; your sins have hidden his face from you' (Isaiah 59:2). Sin also ruptured the relationship between husbands and wives — a rupture often exacerbated by our tendency to justify ourselves. Adam said to God, '"The woman you put here with me — she gave me some fruit from the tree, and I ate it." ... The woman said, "The serpent deceived me, and I ate"' (Genesis 3:12-13).

Competition and jealousy produced alienation between siblings such as Cain and Abel, Abraham and Ishmael, Jacob and Esau. 'Cain was very angry, and his face was downcast' (Genesis 4:5). The same tendency produces dissension between leaders, such as that between Saul and his understudy, David. 'Saul was very angry; this refrain galled him. "They have credited David with tens of thousands," he thought, "but me with only thousands. What more can he get but the kingdom?" And from that time on Saul kept a jealous eye on David' (1 Samuel 18:8-9).

Even in our churches where we ought to celebrate our unity in Christ, we have an inherent tendency to foster conflict. No wonder Paul exhorted: 'Make every effort to keep the unity of the Spirit through the bond of peace' (Ephesians 4:3). In spite of the reality of their redeemed oneness, alienation fractured many early church relationships. Jewish converts looked askance at Gentile disciples. In Corinth believers boasted: '"I follow Paul"; another,"I follow Apollos"; another, "I follow Cephas"; still another, "I follow Christ"' (1 Corinthians 1:12). Paul had to rebuke them severely for the schisms they had introduced into the unity of the church. The wonderful missionary team of Paul and Barnabas was itself broken up because, 'They had such a sharp disagreement that they parted company' (Acts 15:39). To the Philippians Paul wrote: 'I plead with Euodia and I plead with Syntyche to agree with each other in the Lord' (4:2).

Whoever we are, we seem fatally skilled at throwing a wrench into the gears that propel people forward in loving harmony. The wrench may be an angry word or a judgemental comment or an expression of jealousy. Whenever we sense those gears slowing down we need to seek the source, confess our sins and seek forgiveness. Forgiveness is to relationships what WD40 is to shrieking gears. But before we apply the oil of loving forgiveness, we need to extract the cause of the alienation.

The Bible has a lot to say about these causes. James reveals the source of the friction that ignites quarrels. 'What causes fights and quarrels among you? Don't they come from your desires that battle within you? You want something but don't get it. You kill and covet, but you cannot have what you want. You quarrel and fight. You do not have, because you do not ask God … you ask with wrong motives, that you may spend what you get on your pleasures' (James 4:1-3).

The mention of that violent extreme, *killing*, probably distracts most readers from realizing that this passage holds a key to unlock the closet door that hides the machinations of the human heart. God satisfies the legitimate desires we bring to him in prayer. But when someone else blocks illegitimate desires, such as covetousness, passions of anger that lead to quarrelling can easily be aroused. When we do not get what we want we become angry.

The Bible links many violent emotions and actions to greed, covetousness, envy and jealousy. Paul writes of those who turn from God to embrace 'shameful lusts… They have become filled with every kind of wickedness, evil, greed and depravity. They are full of envy, murder, strife, deceit and malice. They are gossips, slanderers, God-haters, insolent, arrogant and boastful; they invent ways of doing evil' (Romans 1:26, 29-30). He lists many other fruits of depravity, but note particularly the proximity of greed, murder, strife, malice, gossip and slander.

In 2 Corinthians Paul expresses his concern lest when he visits them he may find 'quarrelling, jealousy, outbursts of anger, factions, slander, gossip, arrogance and disorder' (12:20). In listing the works of the flesh in Galatians Paul links together 'hatred, discord, jealousy, fits of rage, selfish ambition, dissensions, factions and envy' (5:20-21). In Ephesians he exhorts: 'Get rid of all bitterness, rage and anger, brawling and slander, along with every form of malice' (4:31). In Colossians Paul urges us to stop doing what is natural: 'Put to death, therefore, whatever belongs to your earthly nature' (3:5). This includes inflated desires as well as the 'natural' way we react to grievances (see 3:5-6, 13). That 'natural' way of reacting produces 'anger, rage, malice, slander and filthy language' (3:8).

As linked together in these verses, there are distinct evils that quicken the alienation process:

- greed (inflated desires to acquire something);
- selfish ambition (including insolence, arrogance and boastfulness);
- envy and jealousy;

- anger (along with fits of rage);
- bitterness;
- discord (including strife, factions, disorder, dissensions, brawling);
- slanderous speech (including gossip, slander and filthy language);
- malice (including hatred);
- murder.

Trying to unravel the web of interconnections between our emotions and our sinful desires is notoriously difficult. Nevertheless let me attempt to unravel some of these connections as they relate to the alienation process. Selfishness demands that the desires that feed our ego be met. When these egocentric desires are blocked the result is anger. Anger creates resentment. Resentment leads to bitterness. Resentment may also produce quarrelling. Bitterness may encourage slander or lead to a settled attitude of malice. Malice may inspire the need to get revenge. In extreme cases, the result is murder.

THINK ABOUT IT

Anger is the emotion stirred up when our desires, good or bad, are blocked. Desires may become settled life goals. When someone, or something, prevents us from reaching our goals, the result is anger. Anger retained becomes resentment and bitterness. Resentment may lead to quarrelling, accusations, slander — even physical abuse.

Fortunately, the common grace of God usually prevents people from totally running amok. Common sense leads most to halt obviously self-destructive processes. Fear, or a powerful desire to preserve ourselves — our families, our communities, our countries — moderates how we respond to those who could harm us physically, economically or emotionally. This instinct of self-preservation may be directed towards those who are our own flesh and blood, those who pay our salaries or those in authority over us. An alienated husband may stay with his wife to avoid unfavourable publicity. A worker may swallow his anger at the boss for fear of losing his job. Fear of punishment may stop us from throwing a brick through a neighbour's window.

Social forces rein in our desire to strike out at those who make us angry. If it were otherwise, there would be no corner of the world free from conflict. Thus, most conflict that occurs is covert. Nonetheless, it is very real. Hidden bitterness, resentment or malice becomes the cause of untold human misery. Let us isolate the various elements in this litany of alienation, elements that are linked together in a downward spiral.

Selfish desires

We are selfish from birth. Our self-centred view of life moves us to interpret everything around us in terms of whether or not it bolsters our ego, enhances our image, satisfies our desires or furthers our plans. We are committed to self-protection and self-fulfilment. This is not all bad. Desires, created as they are by God, are not evil in themselves. In prayer we bring genuine needs to God who loves to fulfil them. However, when our desires become overblown, they cause harm. Lust for food can turn to gluttony. Lust for rest may produce laziness. Lust for sex, immorality. Lust for acceptance, bragging and vanity.

Since we are selfish, we unwisely expect those around us to contribute to the fulfilment of our desires. When they do not, we feel the irritation and resentment that initiates the alienation spiral.

Larry Crabb calls this heart-sin 'demandingness'. Speaking of sincere Christians, he writes: 'We are a demanding people... We demand that spouses respond to our needs; we demand that our children exhibit the fruit of our godly training; we demand that our churches be sensitive to our concerns by providing certain ministries; we demand that slow drivers get out of the passing lane; we demand that no one hurt us again the way we were hurt before; we demand that legitimate pleasures, long denied, be ours to enjoy... How absurd! ... Mere people shout orders to the universe,' when we ought to bring our empty cups to God to fill in his way and his time.[2]

The problem with demanding that our desires be met is that we do not live in a castle served by a divine butler. Our desires may conflict with those of others — even harm them. Desires may have to be deferred. We may have to face suffering. God knows what we need to develop Christ-like character; character that cannot be produced if we are catered to like a little baby who gets a bottle every time he cries. Unfortunately, our western democracies intensify this expectation whenever politicians play to the electorate by offering cradle-to-grave care from the government gravy train.

Experience teaches us that we cannot get everything we want. But when we see others around us who have more physical beauty, possessions, image, friends, power or opportunities than we do, our fallen nature moves us to covetousness and envy. Envy leads to jealousy. James warns about harbouring 'bitter envy and selfish ambition in your hearts' (3:14). Failure to destroy envy at its root furthers the alienation process of which James warns.

Anger

Anger is the emotion we feel whenever our desires are blocked. When our lifestyle is criticized, our plans thwarted, our goals blocked, opportunities lost, possessions taken, our reputation minimized, our image marred or our authority challenged, we become angry — to a greater or lesser degree. The frustration we feel is often the result of the actions or comments of other people. But we can just as easily become frustrated over the weather, the breakdown of our car — almost anything.

Whenever we feel anger we should try to discover which of our desires have been challenged or blocked. It may be either a perfectly legitimate aspiration or a sinful lust. The result will be similar whether our blocked desire is for friendship or the sensation of power felt through control of others; whether for unconditional love and respect or the gratification felt from illicit sex; whether for warmth on a cold day or the 'high' experienced through alcohol or drugs; whether for encouragement for a job well done or a proud demand for recognition; whether for a good meal to satisfy our hunger or the gluttony of 'stuffing' ourselves with crisps.

THINK ABOUT IT

> 'We can be angry and not know it. Parents are sometimes deeply resentful of their children, but they hide their resentment behind displays of excessive warmth and disciplined reasonableness. An unplanned child, for example, can cause a parent to struggle terribly with bitterness... Even planned and fully welcome children, when they don't live up to expectations, can provoke disappointment and anger that parents often mask.'
>
> Larry Crabb, *The Real Problem*, p. 79

Blocked desires trigger an unpleasant response within us. That response may be mild irritation or a vague sense of unhappiness. But if we perceive that another person is the cause of the blocked desire, that perception almost inevitably results in resentment and anger. Anger also comes in many forms, from mild irritation to uncontrollable rage. It is often hidden.

In the case of the birth of a child who is not wanted, the blocked goal — to live without the inconvenience of children — is seldom admitted. In the same way, anger may not be recognized when a child fails to live up to a parent's expectations. Unfortunately anger, whether overt or covert, will inevitably produce bitterness or resentment.

The goal we seek could be good, even godly, but to have it blocked still produces irritation or anger that can escalate. Righteous anger occurs when righteous goals are thwarted by evil. We ought to feel anger when injustice prevails in society: when babies are aborted, children are abused, women are beaten by their husbands, employers fail to pay a just wage or when governments persecute Christians. Jesus felt anger at the merchants who had turned the temple into a noisy market. We ought to be outraged when evil men hinder the advance of God's kingdom.

Anger, however, needs to be kept on a short leash. Even righteous anger should not be treasured. It needs to be translated into constructive action. We can divert anger, for example, into positive actions such as evangelism, prayer for unjust men, missionary outreach to countries that persecute Christians, letters written to appeal for justice, establishment of ministries for abused children and women, or opposition to abortion and euthanasia. When we fail to cool our anger it feeds the cycle of alienation.

Resentment, bitterness & depression

Anger that settles into our soul becomes a corrosive feeling harming us and colouring everything we think about the person against whom we harbour the resentment.

Yancey points out that resentment 'means, literally, "to feel again": resentment clings to the past, relives it over and over, picks each fresh scab so that the wound never heals. This pattern doubtless began with the very first couple on earth. "Think of all the squabbles Adam and Eve must have had in the course of their nine hundred years," wrote Martin Luther. "Eve would say, 'You ate the apple,' and Adam would retort, 'You gave it to me.'"'[3]

To harbour grievances, going over them again and again in our minds, distracts us from constructive thought and activity. Resentment fails to achieve any change in the person we resent but it does corrode our own person. Understandable anger can metamorphose into a burning resentment that can swamp our ability to cope with life. As a consequence we harm ourselves and dishonour God.

ILLUSTRATION

Bitterness is closely allied to resentment. It is a more intense and settled disposition of rancour towards those whom we perceive have harmed us. Bitterness distorts our perceptions of others and poisons our own hearts. It spreads beyond its original target to pick new victims — our husband, our children, a neighbour, a co-worker. It conjures up imaginary slights.

Although her parents had apologized to her repeatedly, a woman I'll call Megan could not forgive them for the damage they had caused in her life. In a television 'chat' show I watched, she said, 'I can't forgive them for how they treated me eight years ago.' Her resentment had solidified into an underlying bitterness that corroded every thought she had of her parents. But it had also begun to ruin her marriage, the reason for her presence on the show.

While bitterness tends to poison relationships, it does the most damage to the person who is bitter. Augsburger writes: 'What strange things bitterness can do to us. It slowly sets, like a permanent plaster cast, perhaps protecting the wearer from further pain but ultimately holding the sufferer rigid in frozen animation. Feelings and responses have turned to concrete. Bitterness is paralysis. Bitterness is such a potent paralysis of mind, soul, and spirit that it can freeze reason and emotion. Our attitudes turn cynical, uncaring, critical, and caustic. Where we once ventured to place faith in others, now we trust no one. Optimism darkens to pessimism. Faith grays to doubt.'[4]

THINK ABOUT IT

According to clinical studies, 'Anger has been associated with increased risk of heart attacks and it negatively influences the body's immune system... The psychological benefits [of forgiveness] — including less stress, anxiety and depression — have been widely reported by researchers.'

Julie Sevrens, *Forgiveness is good for you,* Toronto Star, 16 October 1999, p. M18 [byline Palo Alto, Calif.]

Lewis Smedes writes: 'The first person who gains from forgiveness is the person who does the forgiving, and the first person injured by refusal to forgive is the one who was wronged in the first place.'

Smedes, quoted in Gary Thomas, *Forgiveness Factor*, p.10

Lewis Smedes' assertions about forgiveness seemed so self-serving to some theologians that they called his 1984 book, *Forgive and Forget*, a self-centred approach to forgiveness, a kind of 'therapeutic forgiveness'.[5] If our motive for forgiving another is only to relieve our own stress and heal our own emotions, they may have a point. Nevertheless, he is on target in asserting that unforgiveness is self-destructive while forgiveness is personally beneficial to the one who forgives.

ILLUSTRATION

Conflict

Up to this point the process of alienation can, to some extent, be kept under wraps. It has produced resentment and bitterness. It may have become the source of deep depression. Almost certainly, however, what is inside will begin to surface. 2 Corinthians mentions quarrelling, factions and disorder (12:20). Galatians links discord, dissension and factions (5:20-21). James tells us that fights and quarrels — we could include wars — arise when our desires (whether they are personal or international) are blocked. 'You quarrel and fight' because 'you want something but don't get it' (4:2).

A husband drives home expecting a quiet evening of reading. Upon arrival his wife suggests they go out for supper. His dream of a relaxing evening gone, he angrily responds: 'You always want to eat out. Can't you cook a decent meal sometime!' Simmering irritation with his wife flares into open conflict. Stunned at his baseless charge, she cries: 'I've slaved to cook you meals every night this week — lot of thanks I get.'

Consider another scenario. A neighbour thoughtlessly plants a large tree that grows to shade a man's prize rose garden. As the years go by, his resentment grows as his roses deteriorate. One day he decides to put in a high board fence. In the process of putting in the posts, he chops through several of the main roots from his neighbour's tree. His neighbour responds with shouted outrage. Threats and accusations fly back and forth. Conflict is in the open.

A long-time member of a local church loses a vote for a place on the church board. Two years later he and a group of friends stifle a creative proposal promoted by the deacon who beat him in the election. The ensuing conflict threatens to divide the church.

Slander

According to Ephesians, bitterness begins a cycle that progresses to 'rage and anger, brawling and slander' (4:31). Colossians talks of 'lust, evil desires and greed' commencing a cycle that moves on to slander, and filthy language (3:5, 8). James concludes the section we looked at earlier with the exhortation: 'Brothers, do not slander one another' (4:11).

The resentment or bitterness bottled up within bubbles forth as gossip and slander. We just cannot keep our sense of outrage to ourselves. And the story we tell will probably be coloured in such a way that the reputation of the one whom we resent is hurt. Or we may slip gossipy titbits about those who irritate us into conversation. Perversely, we feel justified. After all, aren't we warning others about the subtle dangers they face from this or that person? Besides, harming their reputation is much easier than confrontation. Honest confrontation takes courage! So we use guerrilla tactics.

ILLUSTRATION

No wonder Paul connects the repudiation of anger with the control of our tongue. 'Do not let any unwholesome talk come out of your mouths, but only what is helpful for building others up according to their needs ... do not grieve the Holy Spirit... Get rid of all bitterness, rage and anger...' (Ephesians 4:29-31).

Hatred, malice & revenge

Bitterness spawns hatred. Hatred may either result in a settled desire to avoid the object of one's anger or feed an active longing to see him or her harmed. When bitterness degenerates into malice it becomes dangerous. Every history book records the end result. Every newscast tells a new story.

Colleene Hackett wrote the following to Dr James Dobson, the founder of Focus on the Family: 'In 1991, my beautiful 3½-year-old daughter was accidentally shot in the head and killed by the 8-year-old boy next door. Needless to say, my life came to a screeching halt. My daughter lay dead in my front yard, and my 5-year-old son had witnessed the whole thing. My life went from normal and routine and beautiful to a complete mess, filled with psychiatrists for both my son and myself — as well as plotting and planning how I would kill not only the little boy who shot my daughter, but also the entire family. I felt justified. I felt that I should do it.'[6]

Colleene Hackett's outrage over the shooting of her daughter led from anger to hatred to malice. She felt justified in wreaking vengeance on the whole family — for an accident. When the desire for vengeance consumes us, we are driven by the determination to see the cause of our anguish suffer as we have suffered.

The only way to get off this 'down escalator' leading from anger to murder is to forgive one's enemies, to do good to those who harm us. At a meeting of the American Psychological Association, Harden suggested that 'forgiveness, not retaliation, "represents the most strategic intervention in reducing violence in our society"'.[7]

The cycle of alienation

A blocked desire leads to irritation and anger. Anger harboured produces resentment. Resentment feeds bitterness. Bitterness can provoke conflict or slander. Bitterness further metamorphoses into hatred and malice. Malice fires vengeance, which may even result in violence and murder.

If we are to escape this escalator, we must recognize the various stages through which it passes in its descent towards open violence. A blocked desire leads to irritation and anger. Anger that is harboured produces resentment. Resentment feeds bitterness. It can provoke conflict or slander. Bitterness metamorphoses into hatred and malice. Malice fires vengeance.

ILLUSTRATION

How does this all work out in real life? I'm using another extreme example of the alienation cycle in the hope that, when we view it operating on a scale beyond what most of us will ever experience, we will recognize its extreme danger.

Sydna Massé lived next door to Diane, her husband Brian and their three children. During chats and walks with Diane and her family, Sydna came to realize that Diane loved the Lord. Although ever since a teenage abortion she had felt estranged from God, she longed for the peace that Diane enjoyed. To her shock, and that of the whole community, one day Jennie, who was having an affair with Diane's husband, killed Diane and fled. A badly planned escape led to her arrest and a quick trial, followed by imprisonment for both Brian and Jennie.

Jennie, the murderess, became the object of Sydna's consuming hatred. In describing her condition, Gary Thomas writes: 'Sydna grew "physically hot" when the murderer's name — Jennifer — was even mentioned or her picture was flashed on television. "I couldn't even read the newspaper articles," she admits. "I had a dead friend and now lived behind three motherless kids. I felt I had every right to hate the murderer who caused this… There was no relief in her sentencing. That's the thing with hatred and bitterness — it eats you alive. Every time I passed the house, I missed Diane and became angry all over again.'"[8]

Shortly after the murder of her friend, Sydna joined a Bible study group where she confronted the Christian teaching on forgiveness. She writes: 'I asked God whom I needed to forgive ... I did not want the answer I got: Jennie (the murderess). I pleaded, "Lord, she killed a mother of three and my friend!"'[9]

As she agonized over this challenge, she remembered that she had aborted her first child. She realized that, in God's sight, she too was a murderess. She continues her story: 'It became obvious that the Lord wanted me not only to forgive Jennie but to reach out to her. Writing my first letter to her was difficult. I was a stranger, and any such letter asking for forgiveness needed to be carefully worded. When I placed the letter in the mailbox, peace filled me. My anger was gone and I understood why God makes forgiveness such a high priority in the Christian's life. Anger and bitterness hurt us more than the ones they are directed against.'[10]

We can certainly relate to Sydna's anger. Surely she was justified in feeling this way towards her friend's murderess? But as her story demonstrates, anger usually escalates into rage, corrosive hatred and a settled feeling of bitterness. It may lead to a consuming malice that even results in murder. Clearly, we must ask God to arrest the alienation process before it has a chance to destroy our lives.

DISCUSS IT

QUESTIONS FOR DISCUSSION

1. *Read James 3:13 – 4:4. James writes that a life marked by heavenly wisdom is characterized by purity, harmony in relationships (peace-loving), thoughtfulness towards others (considerate), respect for others (submissive), mercy, impartiality, sincerity and all kinds of good fruit or deeds.*
   a. *What are the outward signs of a life marked by earthly wisdom?*
   b. *What are the inner attitudes that energize the person marked by heavenly wisdom?*
   c. *What are the inner attitudes (emotions/ motives) that energize the person marked by earthly wisdom?*

2. *Heavenly wisdom then, produces harmony in relationships, while earthly wisdom injects conflict. At its root, in us, what is the real source of conflict (quarrels, fights, alienation)?*

3. *Explain how pride promotes alienation and conflict while humility fosters harmony (see 3:13; 4:6, 10).*

4. *In Galatians 5:19-21 we read that the 'acts of the sinful nature are … hatred, discord, jealousy, fits of rage, selfish ambition, dissensions, factions and envy'. In Ephesians 4:31 we are urged to 'Get rid of all bitterness, rage and anger,*

brawling and slander, along with every form of malice.' Using the words of these verses list the various steps in the cycle of alienation from its origin in attitudes to its culmination in violent action.

5. *Give practical examples that illustrate how a frustrated, or blocked, desire can lead to alienation or conflict.*

6. *In chapter four, verse three, James explains that the wrong kind of prayer can be a part of this whole cycle of increasing alienation. Write out a prayer that you could offer to God that would lead you to avoid the frustration that often leads to conflict.*

CHAPTER SIX

PREPARING FOR FORGIVENESS

LOOK IT UP

BIBLE REFERENCE

'Search me, O God, and know my heart;
test me and know my anxious thoughts.
See if there is any offensive way in me,
and lead me in the way everlasting'
(Psalm 139:23-24).

INTRODUCTION

In recent years trying to grow tomatoes has made me rather frustrated. After the first flush of growth my tomato plants would begin to die back from the bottom up. No one I asked provided a satisfactory explanation until one garden consultant inquired if I had black walnut trees in the vicinity. 'Well, yes,' I answered, 'I've planted several within fifty feet or so.' The consultant explained that black walnut trees spread a toxin through the soil that kills tomatoes. She suggested that I either move the garden, get rid of the walnut trees or plant the tomatoes in raised beds beyond the reach of the toxins. I chose the last option. This year my tomatoes flourished.

Bitterness is a deadly toxin that poisons relationships. Before we can attempt to bring reconciliation to others, we must be sure that our own hearts are right. If our hearts are bitter or resentful, attempts at reconciliation are liable to worsen the problem.

In this chapter, I share several questions that I ask myself periodically in an attempt to maintain good relationships. Careful attention to these questions should prepare us to be the peacemakers that we have been redeemed to become.

1. Am I proud?

When we react to others with unreasonable anger, the cause can sometimes be traced to a sense of superiority. Commonly, we have an exaggerated opinion of ourselves — what fine Christians we are, how valuable our time is, how important our plans are, why priority should be given to our desires. When this is the case, the first thing we need to do is to confess our egotism to the Holy Spirit.

Hypocrisy is a universal human problem, a latent tendency we explored in chapter two. We are good at seeing the speck in our brother's eye, even when we have a plank in our own. Clearly, we cannot become sincerely forgiving people unless God gives us a glimpse of our depravity in his mirror.

The psalmist realized our inability to be honest about ourselves. 'Who can discern his errors?' (Psalm 19:12). Because of this tendency, he prayed, 'Search me, O God, and know my heart; test me and know my anxious thoughts. See if there is any offensive way in me, and lead me in the way everlasting' (Psalm 139:23-24). Fleeing the horror of hypocrisy, the sensitive believer beseeches God to expose offensive thoughts, words and deeds. Once they are acknowledged, he appeals for the Holy Spirit's help in adopting a lifestyle free from their poison.

The offensive ways discovered may include deeply buried bitterness, anger, envy, jealousy and even hatred. These destructive emotions may seem to be justified, rooted in the memories of bad experiences that occurred decades ago. No matter what the source, we must deliberately choose to stop playing the 'victim game'. If we cherish evil emotions, we choose evil. Evil must be confessed to God and abandoned with revulsion. When we confess these transgressions of his law of love to our Father we know that 'he will forgive us our sins and purify us from all unrighteousness' (1 John 1:9).

Confession paves the way to the conquest of pride. Reconcilers are humble people. Not that they are conscious of this quality. They are often painfully aware of their sinfulness and dependence on the mercy of God. We cannot create humility. A daily devotional exposure to the Scriptures will do much to develop the personal honesty that undergirds biblical humility. Ultimately, however, humility is more a quality produced in us by the Holy Spirit as he helps us to become more vulnerable and honest about ourselves.

When Sydna Massé (mentioned in the previous chapter) joined a Bible study she came face to face with her own sin. She had aborted a child. That realization destroyed the imagined moral high ground from whose height she could look down with righteous anger on her friend's murderess. She suddenly realized that she herself was guilty of murder in the sight of God. This new realism — call it humility — opened the door to forgiveness.

Notice how conflict with the old nature leads to avoidance of conceit in the following passage: 'Live by the Spirit, and you will not gratify the desires of the sinful nature. For the sinful nature desires what is contrary to the Spirit, and the Spirit what is contrary to the sinful nature. They are in conflict with each other ... let us keep in step with the Spirit. Let us not be conceited, provoking and envying each other' (Galatians 5:16-17, 25).

The passage in Ephesians 6 referring to the Christian's armour unveils the believer's continual warfare (vv. 10-20). This conflict is not with other people. It rages in the soul, where we struggle to put off our 'old self, which is being corrupted by its deceitful desires' (4:22). Targeted as we are by the enemy who probes for any weakness, we cannot drop our guard or decide to take a month's vacation from spiritual conflict.

This danger should lead us to keep very close to the cross. 'If anyone would come after me, he must deny himself and take up his cross daily and follow me' (Luke 9:23). Daily cross-bearing means a daily crucifixion of our self-centred nature with all its attendant evils.

Could the difficulty some have in forgiving others be traced to their lack of understanding of this conflict?

Maybe they have given up the fight? Certainly, many professing believers seem to have retreated from the battlefield. If so, the pride that makes them condemn others so readily is understandable, though not acceptable. There is nothing like blindness to our own sins to make us self-righteous.

THINK ABOUT IT

My heart was heavy, for its trust had been
Abused, its kindness answered with foul wrong;
So, turning gloomily from my fellowmen,
One summer Sabbath day I strolled among
The green mounds of the village burial-place;
Where pondering how all human love and hate
Find one sad level; and how, soon or late,
Wronged and wrongdoer, each with meekened
face,
And cold hands folded over a still heart,
Pass the green threshold of our common grace,
Whither all footsteps tend, whence none depart,
Awed for myself, and pitying my race,
Our common sorrow, like a mighty wave
Swept all my pride away, and trembling I forgave.

John Greenleaf Whittier, cited in Herbert V. Prochnow & Herbert V. Prochnow Jr, *A Treasure Chest of Quotations for All Occasions*, New York: Harper & Row, 1983, p.362.

2. Am I assured of God's love?

Our sins cling to us like leeches. With Paul we cry: 'What a wretched man I am! Who will rescue me?' (Romans 7:24). Far from leading us to go through life wallowing in thoughts of our own iniquity, the Spirit — as we saw in chapter three — calls us to rejoice in God's love.

Our rescue comes not from turning over a new leaf. Not from trying harder. Not even from more Bible reading. Nor some second blessing. What we need is a liberating sense of the gospel of grace. We should be able to cry: 'Thanks be to God — through Jesus Christ our Lord!' (Romans 7:25). God sprinkles the salt of the gospel on these bloodsuckers, our sins, and they recoil in anguish. We are free!

Through the promptings of the Holy Spirit we put our faith in the good news of Jesus Christ who died for our sins, was buried and rose again the third day. The blood of Christ propitiates the wrath of God. We have been rescued by the love of God!

We need to rest in that love. Unfortunately, like the foolish Galatians, we keep straying from a celebration of God's free grace (see Galatians 1:6; 3:1-5). Steeped as we are in a culture that buttresses our independence and tries to enhance our sense of self-worth in foolish ways, we drift back into attempts to earn our standing with God. Even our struggles to live the Christian life become self-absorbed. Inevitable failures lead to frustration. When we look around and see others who seem to be successful, our disappointment with ourselves breeds envy or irritation. We rationalize. We try to bring others down to our level. No wonder relationships suffer. When we stop resting in God's gracious love, we stop offering revolutionary forgiveness.

David Seamands, a counsellor, writes: 'Many years ago I was driven to the conclusion that the two major causes of most emotional problems among evangelical Christians are these: the failure to understand, receive, and live out God's unconditional grace and forgiveness; and the failure to give out that unconditional love, forgiveness, and grace to other people.'[1]

In prison Paul knelt before the Father and prayed for the Ephesians: 'that you, being rooted and established in love, may have power, together with all the saints, to grasp how wide and long and high and deep is the love of Christ ... that surpasses knowledge — that you may be filled to the measure of all the fulness of God' (3:17-19).

We need to lean back and rest in the Father's love. 'If God is for us, who can be against us? He who did not spare his own Son, but gave him up for us all — how will he not also, along with him, graciously give us all things? ... Who shall separate us from the love of Christ? ... For I am convinced that neither death nor life, neither angels nor demons, neither the present nor the future, nor any powers, neither height nor depth, nor anything else in all creation, will be able to separate us from the love of God that is in Christ Jesus our Lord' (Romans 8:31-32, 38-39).

Wow! To think that we are bound to God by cords of indestructible love. That knowledge ought to make us dance around our living room! With so much love pouring into our hearts we ought to have much left over to share with others.

3. Am I submissive to God's will?

Since we are human, things happen that shake us up so badly that our eyes drift from Christ to agonize over our circumstances. Often the cause can be found in the actions of other people. People upset our lives and destroy our plans. We lose a job through a colleague's cheating. Our car is wrecked when another drives through a stop sign. Another woman steals our husband.

Terrible events intersect our lives. The Christian, however, is not adrift in a flimsy canoe always threatened by the wake thrown up by someone else's power cruiser. Part of denying ourselves and taking up our cross daily involves committing our plans to God. Romans 12 exhorts us: 'in view of God's mercy, to offer your bodies as living sacrifices, holy and pleasing to God — this is your spiritual act of worship' (v. 1).

The pattern of many, to motor through life with a determined competitiveness, following a compass direction set by their own goals, results in frequent collisions with others. Such an approach leaves a lot of anger and bitterness in its wake.

By submitting to God, the obedient Christian is 'able to test and approve what God's will is — his good, pleasing and perfect will' (Romans 12:2). By trusting in God's sovereign governance of the universe, the Christian can avoid the resentment that events and people cause. Although, like Job, he will not always understand God's leading he can trust in the knowledge 'that in all things God works for the good of those who love him, who have been called according to his purpose' (Romans 8:28). That trust enables him to endure 'trouble or hardship or persecution or famine or nakedness or danger or sword... In all these things we are more than conquerors through him who loved us' (Romans 8:35, 37).

This is no easy believism. It's tough. But the alternative is to perceive life as a series of chaotic events produced by 'blind fate'. In reality, providence, not fate, governs. God rules the universe, upholding all things by the word of his power. We desperately need faith in God's providential ability to overrule the worst events for our good and his glory.

As I was writing these words the phone rang. An angel was on the other end. Her name is Jessie, a woman who is ninety-one years old. She had called to encourage me concerning another book I had written. Her call was supernatural! Why? Well, throughout the conversation she exuded cheerfulness. And yet, when I probed, I discovered that the previous week she had suffered a fall leaving her incapacitated and dependent on others. She expressed thankfulness for the help of those who came to give her therapy, wash her and feed her. Her only complaint was that it was a bit difficult to get from her wheelchair into a taxi so she could visit her bedridden husband in the hospital!

Len, her husband, is similarly blessed with the joy of the Lord. To my astonishment, I learned that two weeks previously he had fallen out of bed when someone forgot to put up its sides. He lay on the floor, helpless, until a nurse discovered him.

I must admit that, given that pair of experiences, I would probably be angry, frustrated and depressed. I would be breathing threats at the hospital administration. Jessie and Len seem to take it all in their stride. They cannot understand why people who face minor inconveniences aren't as cheerful as they are. Both have gone through some very bad times. Both have learned to trust in God's providence and to love each other unconditionally.

But I need to ask myself another question.

4. Do I accept my own uniqueness?

All of us are different. Some are handsome, others a little plump and bald. Some are beautiful; others have features that cry out for the cartoonist's pencil. Some have the 'gift of the gab' while most of us are plodding conversationalists. Some are brilliant in maths — others in woodworking. Some get ahead. Some are stalled in

EXPLANATION

dead-end jobs. Most of us are ordinary, very ordinary.

These differences can get us down. As we look around at others we feel a little bit jealous of their popularity, attractiveness, or success. As we read about business tycoons, sports' heroes and Hollywood stars we may daydream about what it would be like to have more money, a slimmer build, a more attractive face.

Now a healthy vision of what we can become through taking steps to develop in different areas is good. Morbid dissatisfaction with ourselves and our lot, however, spawns empty daydreams. They, in turn, can produce envy. Envy sets the stage for resentment and bitterness.

The antidote to envy is acceptance of the way God has made us. We need to rejoice in the 'glory of his grace, by which He made us accepted in the Beloved' (Ephesians 1:6, NJKV). After all, God chose, predestined, adopted and redeemed us (see Ephesians 1:4-14). Isn't failure to accept ourselves tantamount to questioning God's integrity in choosing us?

Besides our spiritual identity in Christ, he has given us spiritual gifts uniquely chosen to suit our personality. Gifts of the Spirit endow us with the skills needed to find our niche in the kingdom. Paul urges us not to think of ourselves boastfully but 'rather think of yourself with sober judgement … we have different gifts according to the grace given us' (Romans 12:3, 6). In

Corinthians he writes: 'Now to each one the manifestation of the Spirit is given for the common good... He gives them to each one, just as he determines. The body is a unit, though it is made up of many parts ... those parts of the body that seem to be weaker are indispensable' (1 Corinthians 12:7, 11-12, 22). In describing the interdependence of the parts of a body, Paul illustrates how essential each of us is to the church. Whether our gift is preaching or practical help we are equally important to Christ and essential for the smooth functioning of the body.

THINK ABOUT IT

When someone calls you ugly — and it doesn't matter!

'When you don't have any agenda but Jesus' agenda and you know that Jesus is Lord, you don't have to be uptight. When the essence of one's teaching is that we are a lot worse than we think we are and God's grace is a lot bigger than we think it is; that we are really messed-up folks whom a sovereign God has, for His own reasons, decided to love unconditionally; that grace always runs downhill; and that power is really made perfect in weakness ... you can hardly get upset with others... In other words, if someone calls you ugly, and you know you're ugly and don't care, it doesn't matter for him or her to say so.'

Steve Brown, *Key Life Network Ministry Letter*, August 2000

ILLUSTRATION

The value God puts upon us counts more than the opinion of all the queens, prime ministers and presidents put together. Of course, if we accept God's opinion of us, we will not have to win every argument.

5. Am I argumentative?

Allied with a failure to understand how precious we are in the sight of God is a sense of inferiority that may lead us to be argumentative. Can we accept others, their immaturity or maturity in Christ, even their opinions? If we feel insecure, others may threaten us. We will either retreat into passivity and silence or pursue an aggressive stance in an attempt to prove them wrong. This may manifest itself in an argumentative spirit that deepens conflict.

A pastor mistakenly quotes the wrong reference in a sermon. We feel duty-bound to correct him after the service. We interrupt our adult Sunday school teacher to point out something he or she missed in the text. In a social gathering we break into a story told by another about their summer vacation to upstage him with news about a bear we spotted on our vacation. We feel duty bound to correct another Christian's statement about 'free will'. Are we always arguing about the second coming of Christ, supralapsarianism, reformed theology?

I'm not talking here about never correcting false doctrine. That needs to be approached gently and privately in the way Priscilla and Aquila did with Apollos. 'They invited him to their home and explained to him the way of God more adequately' (Acts 18:26). No, the questions that I need to ask myself at this point are: 'Do I tend to interrupt people? Correct people in public? Argue about things concerning which there are valid differences of opinion? Do I have to get "my two pence worth" in every conversation? Do I feel threatened by others with more exciting experiences, more knowledge in a certain area, or more ability to secure attention in conversations?'

If I am argumentative, let me ask the Holy Spirit to make me more secure in who he has made me, more gracious, more patient with others. But let me ask myself another question.

6. Am I content?

I'm not talking here about being content with our progress in Christ. No, like Paul we should be able to say, 'Not that I have already obtained all this, or have already been made perfect; but I press on' (Philippians 3:12). We are urged to keep on pursuing 'righteousness, godliness, faith, love, endurance and gentleness' (1 Timothy 6:11).

Rather, the question concerns contentment with our lot in life: our house, bank account, clothing, car. Lack of contentment here breeds envy.

'But godliness with contentment is great gain. For we brought nothing into the world, and we can take nothing out of it. But if we have food and clothing, we will be content with that. People who want to get rich fall into temptation and a trap and into many foolish and harmful desires that plunge men into ruin and destruction. For the love of money is a root of all kinds of evil. Some people, eager for money, have wandered from the faith and pierced themselves with many griefs' (1 Timothy 6:6-10).

This is not a problem unique to the upwardly mobile. Poor people can easily feed their discontent by envying those with abundant money who drive a Mercedes and eat in luxurious restaurants. As a missionary and pastor, living on a limited income, I have sometimes found myself becoming angry with well-off Christians in a position to increase my salary. It's hard to be content in a day when billions of dollars go into creating advertising that will breed discontent. But contentment is a great antidote to envy. Freedom from envy starves the resentment that feeds conflict.

7. Do I have a disciplined approach to anger?

A car cuts me off on the roadway. My husband gives me the silent treatment. Dad misjudges my motives. Another woman cheats her way into a promotion at work. We are kept waiting three hours with a very sick child in the emergency room of the hospital. A friend wrongly accuses me of gossip.

Interruptions; irritations; misunderstandings; injustice; thoughtlessness; selfishness; cruelty; inconveniences. Since we live east of Eden, our lives often intersect with events and people who arouse our ire. We never know when something will spark our anger. So, we ought to have anger-extinguishing equipment handy to douse the sudden fires that flare into life. What can we do to prepare that equipment?

THINK ABOUT IT

One morning Ralph Milton was awakened at five o'clock by a terrible racket on his roof. Going out to investigate he found a woodpecker pounding away on the metal TV antenna. Angry at this interruption in his sleep, Ralph threw a rock at the creature. The rock sailed over the house and hit his car with a crash. In anger he took a vicious kick at a clod of dirt, only to remember — too late — that he was still in his bare feet!

As told by Jim Taylor in *Currents*, date unknown

First of all, we need to remind ourselves what the Bible says about anger. Anger can be righteous. Jesus was angry with the merchants in the temple. We should expect to become angry when we see evil promoted, when a lie is proclaimed as truth, when an injustice occurs. Speaking of this kind of anger, Ephesians says,

'In your anger do not sin. Do not let the sun go down while you are still angry, and do not give the devil a foothold' (4:26-27).

Since anger is a powerful emotion, it destabilizes the soul, making it hard for the mind to think rationally. And if evil is to be stopped, it will be stopped through careful thought, not unthinking outbursts of wrath or burning resentment that continues day after day. For this reason, even righteous anger needs to be reigned in.

Secondly, we need to develop self-control. While we cannot stop involuntary feelings of anger from arising within, we can moderate their intensity by developing self-control. 'A hot-tempered man stirs up dissension, but a patient man calms a quarrel' (Proverbs 15:18). 'Do not be quickly provoked in your spirit, for anger resides in the lap of fools' (Ecclesiastes 7:9). Patience moderates our response to provocation.

We should pray earnestly for the Holy Spirit to use every irritation as an occasion to develop within us a reasoned approach to conflict. Ultimately, dealing with anger is a choice of the will. Dr Dobson writes: 'The exercise of the will stands in the gap between the two halves of the verse: "Be angry" and "sin not".'[2]

Self-control is one of the fruits of the Holy Spirit's activity. The more we ask him to help us react patiently to minor irritations, the more we will be ready to endure major provocations without losing control.

8. Do I have the courage to confront or confess?

Exercising humility and self-control does not mean we will not be called to face those who were the cause of our anguish or the victims of our sin. Initiating the forgiveness process will require someone to take the initiative: the offended party, the one who caused the offence or a mediator (see chapter 8). This is not easy.

Bringing a person, or group, face-to-face with past anguish may backfire. They may become belligerent and antagonistic. People tend to avoid dealing with unpleasant truths. In spite of the potential for unpleasantness, we have a Christian responsibility to humbly and graciously confront the source of the alienation. 'Brothers, if someone is caught in a sin, you who are spiritual should restore him gently' (Galatians 6:1).

Most of Paul's epistles dealt with problems that had arisen in new churches. He demonstrated considerable courage in laying out in black and white the nature of each schism, each heresy, each aberration. Then he followed up his letters with visits.

The offending party will need courage also. Jesus taught that if we remember that a brother has something against us, we should immediately 'go and be reconciled' (Matthew 5:24). It is never easy to go to a person we have hurt, confess our offence and seek their forgiveness. We tend to squirm, to rehearse all the reasons why we shouldn't go, to rationalize our desire to 'let sleeping dogs lie' lest they wake and bite us.

ILLUSTRATION

9. Do I trust in God's justice?

Verdell Goulding writes that, 'As the very nature of forgiveness is to forgo revenge when the wrongdoer's actions deserve it, the necessity to forgive is completely opposed to our innate need to see justice administered. This places most people in a psychological dilemma — we want to forgive, yet forgiveness seems unfair because the wrongdoer does not deserve it.'[3]

Lewis Smedes comments: 'Some people view forgiveness as a cheap avoidance of justice, a plastering over of wrong, a sentimental make-believe. If forgiveness is a whitewashing of wrong, then it is itself wrong. Nothing that whitewashes evil can be good. It can be good only if it is a redemption from the effects of evil, not a make-believing that the evil never happened.'[4]

Robert Enright notes: 'Forgiveness does not mean you forgo justice. People are responsible for their actions, whether those actions are committed in Yugoslavia or in an elected official's private office.'[5]

Clearly forgiveness is not a way to avoid confronting and clarifying evil. 'Forgiveness involves taking the offense seriously, not passing it off as inconsequential or insignificant.'[6] It does not deny the validity of the civil justice system. But whatever the courts, or any individual, may attempt, genuine forgiveness cannot occur without the redemptive activity of God. He is the moral centre of the universe. He alone can cut through the moral fog that surrounds events to right wrongs.

We need to trust him. Otherwise what alternative do we have? Engage in civil disobedience? Protest against lenient courts? Plan revenge — the hounding of perpetrators to the ends of the earth — the stuff of popular novels? We cannot say what we would do in the place of Jewish survivors of Auschwitz, or Tutsis in Rwanda, or bereaved parents in Peru, or burnt-out church members in Indonesia. But we do know that vengeance never evens the score.

The message of Jesus calls a halt to the escalating cost of vengeance. 'You have heard that it was said, "Eye for eye, and tooth for tooth." But I tell you, Do not resist an evil person. If someone strikes you on the right cheek, turn to him the other also... Love your enemies and pray for those who persecute you' (Matthew 5:38-39, 44). Paul reiterates the teaching of our Lord: 'Do not repay anyone evil for evil... If it is possible, as far as it depends on you, live at peace with everyone. Do not take revenge, my friends, but leave room for God's wrath, for it is written: "It is mine to avenge; I will repay," says the Lord... Do not be overcome by evil, but overcome evil with good' (Romans 12:17-19, 21).

When we take vengeance, we usurp the role of God and allow ourselves to be overcome by evil. By forgiving our enemies, we overcome evil with good. How can we do this? Jesus commands us to love our enemies by praying for them. Deliverance from vengeance begins in prayer. Prayer connects us to the God of both justice and mercy who alone can soften an enemy's heart.

Choosing to give gifts to those who harm us accelerates deliverance. Applying the teaching of Christ and quoting Proverbs, Paul exhorts us, 'If your enemy is hungry, feed him; if he is thirsty, give him something to drink. In doing this you will heap burning coals on his head' (Romans 12:20). While we might not give those who harm us food or water, we could write them a note or even give them a gift. Giving to those who harm us is so unnatural that it is like fire to their souls. God may use this shock to their system, to shame them into abandoning their aggression.

TO SUMMARIZE

Questions I ask myself

1. Am I proud?
2. Am I assured of God's love?
3. Am I submissive to God's will?
4. Do I accept my own uniqueness?
5. Am I argumentative?
6. Am I content?
7. Do I have a disciplined approach to anger?
8. Do I have the courage to confront or confess?
9. Do I trust in God's justice?

When we revoke any attempt to get back at the person, or group, who has wronged us, we do not abandon justice. No, we turn the case over to God. How he chooses to right the wrong is his business. In the meantime, he has committed to us the ministry of reconciliation. That means embracing mercy, and showing love. Perhaps, the love of God that pursued us will woo those who have harmed us as well. How much better to be an instrument of peace than a weapon of war!

In China in 1949, when he was seventeen, Paul Chang's parents urged him to flee the country. He caught the last train before the Communists overran his family's place of refuge. Paul never saw his father, Pastor Chang, again. His father was arrested, brainwashed, tortured and starved in an attempt to force him to recant his faith. Although his body was broken, his life radiated 'a prayer of compassion until he died'.[7]

Paul has every reason to hate his father's captors. Instead he uses his gifts in meetings throughout Asia to sing and testify of the forgiving grace of God. 'No trace of bitterness lingers in his heart. Only the light of forgiveness shines through his words and songs... Paul explains: "Forgiveness comes from what I have experienced through God, because He has forgiven me... If I did not have the spirit of forgiveness, I could not preach the Gospel as a servant of Christ."'[8]

Several years ago Paul, with his wife and children, returned to China to visit his eighty-three-year-old mother and his four brothers and their families. They told him how his father died, then they all went to see his grave. 'Tears of pain held back for decades brimmed over while the brothers took turns praying. As the healing power of forgiveness filled their hearts, the realization swept over them that hatred and resentment would only limit God's use of their gifts and talents.'[9]

Instead of joining Chinese freedom fighters seeking revenge, Paul joined the gospel's freedom train. So must we.

QUESTIONS FOR DISCUSSION

DISCUSS IT

1. Do either A or B.

A. Read the following verses and match them to the questions below: Ephesians 4:26-27; Galatians 6:1; Romans 12:1-2; 8:31-35; 12:17-19; Philippians 4:11-13; James 4:6; 2 Timothy 2:23-24; 1 Corinthians 12:4-7, 27.

B. Read Romans 12. There is much teaching in this chapter that is not specifically related to establishing a climate conducive to forgiveness; however, much is relevant. Opposite each of the questions below, copy any teaching that is relevant to that particular question.

a. Am I proud?
b. Am I assured of God's love?
c. Am I submissive to God's will?
d. Do I accept my own uniqueness?
e. Am I argumentative?

f. Am I content?
g. Do I have a disciplined approach to anger?
h. Do I have the courage to confront or confess?
i. Do I trust in God's justice?

2. *Find a biblical character, besides Christ, who positively exemplifies the character qualities represented by each of these questions.*

3. *Which questions do you find hardest to answer positively?*

4. *Spend time in prayer asking God to help you in any area where a need is exposed.*

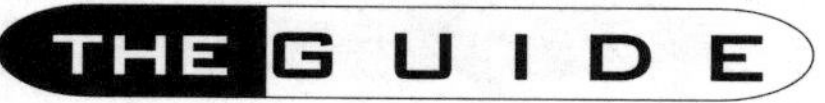

CHAPTER SEVEN

FORGIVENESS: WHAT IT IS AND WHAT IT ISN'T

LOOK IT UP

BIBLE REFERENCE

'Bear with each other and forgive whatever grievances you may have against one another. Forgive as the Lord forgave you' (Colossians 3:13).

INTRODUCTION

Before we can define forgiveness positively, we need to consider it negatively — what it isn't. We often confuse forgiveness with forbearance. Let me explain.

Janice lost the chance to get a great job when her husband Marv failed to mail the application she had so laboriously prepared. When Marv discovered the letter under a pile of second-class mail on his desk, the deadline was past. He was devastated by his carelessness. He tried to apologize but it was too late. Janice was furious. When Janice accused Marv of not wanting her to get a job outside the home Marv felt defensive. He responded by calling her a 'picky perfectionist'. Their marriage deteriorated.

What should her Christian response have been? One can certainly understand Janice's keen disappointment. Should she have forgiven Marv? If he had deliberately avoided mailing her letter, we can understand that forgiveness would be needed. Or if he made a habit of being careless and took no pains to develop discipline, we might classify his action as a temperamental sin for which he needed forgiveness. Forgiveness is needed where sin is committed. But in this instance Marv was not sinfully chauvinistic, just careless. Janice should have exercised forbearance.

Forbearance is often confused with forgiveness. Sins require forgiveness but inadequacies due to human frailty, even oversights due to carelessness, call for forbearance.

Janice's response was sinful. Her anger with Marv was based on judgement of his motives. Marv responded in kind. An unfortunate failure on Marv's part, forgetting to mail the letter, led to a hurtful cycle of alienation. Relational friction is often caused by human frailty. Although the antecedent of angry words is often innocent and non-moral, the result can degenerate into moral and relational evil: bitter words, resentment, divorce. Where we fail, either to allow leeway for human fallibility, or to grant too much credence to imagination, the results can be deadly.

Friction may be due to a clash of temperaments. One person may take considerable time to think through decisions and even after deciding moves slowly. When this phlegmatic type of person is married to, or works with, an irascible person who is decisive and driving, their contrasting approaches create frustration. Lifestyles and temperaments vary widely. The differences generated are not due to sin, just personality.

The call to forbearance is clear. 'Be completely humble and gentle; be patient, bearing with one another in love' (Ephesians 4:2). 'Bear with each other'

EXPLANATION

(Colossians 3:13). Humility, gentleness and patience enable us to love people with their human imperfections without getting angry and annoyed. Humility is based on both a realization of how far short we fall from God's standards and a realistic assessment of our own foibles. Gentleness leads us to treat others with a measure of the thoughtfulness God lavishes on us. Patience develops as we rejoice in God's longsuffering and recognize how we strain each other's patience.

Matthew Henry comments that 'It becomes those who are holy towards God to be lowly and loving towards all men.' He goes on to say, 'Mutual forbearance [is needed] in consideration of the infirmities and deficiencies under which we all labour... We have all of us something which needs to be borne with, and this is a good reason why we should bear with others in what is disagreeable to us. We need the same good turn from others which we are bound to show them.'[1]

Patient forbearance is called for in the face of:

- Unintentional mistakes;
- Accidents;
- Fancied slights or imagined motives;
- Human foibles such as clumsiness, forgetfulness, carelessness, etc.;
- Physical infirmities such as hearing loss, poor eyesight, etc.;

- Valid differences of opinion;
- Cultural differences;
- Questionable practices concerning which genuine Christians have differing opinions;
- Differences of temperament and emphasis;
- Differences in Christian maturity.

If we fail to develop enough humility to realize that we all share a multitude of human failings, we may become as critical as Virginia. 'Virginia thinks pointing out a problem is solving it. She feels she is doing some great thing for God by spotting a need. She doesn't understand that meeting one need is more important than spotting fifty.'[2] Virginia belongs to the professional critics' union composed of those adept at finding problems in any proposal, flaws in any person — but who are blind to their own foibles.

Forbearance not only rescues us from being judgemental but it prepares us to handle human diversity. Often the antagonism that springs up in our churches can be traced to a failure to bear with differences of opinion. One wants more choruses while another complains about the dearth of grand old hymns. One faction urges quiet in the sanctuary; the other promotes fellowship through friendly conversation. And money! Some want to put a budget surplus into a guarantee investment while others agitate for sending the balance to missionaries. The issues may be important or trivial. Reactions are often heated. But in most cases what is called for is the ability to bear with those who differ.

ILLUSTRATION

Relational friction may also be rooted in imaginary grievances. Too often we attribute motives to others based on our analysis of why they act in a certain way. Instead of confronting the person we imagine has treated us shabbily or cutting off all fellowship with them, what is needed is for us to 'cast down imaginations'. God is omniscient. We are not!

A certain woman developed a growing animosity towards a former close friend. Imagined slights poisoned the relationship. One of the few things that brought sunshine into her drab life was a 'secret pal' who remembered her birthdays and anniversaries and, in other thoughtful ways, cheered her up.

Finally, her estranged friend died. In spite of her bitterness, the woman thought that ordinary decency required her to make a neighbourly call on the grieving husband. She offered to help him straighten up the house. While tidying up, she found a letter addressed to her. Opening it, she discovered — to her shock — that the 'secret pal' who had brought such encouragement into her gloomy life was none other than the target of her animosity! Thoughts of the years of maligning and misjudging this former friend filled her with grief. Forbearance rescues us from this kind of unnecessary suffering. It steers us away from the relational crash that follows an inability to bear with the shortcomings of others.

Apologies

While circumstances that call for forbearance do not require the exercise of forgiveness, they often do call for an apology. If Marv had sincerely apologized to Janice for failing to mail her letter, she might have responded differently. 'Honey, I'm really sorry. I knew how much that letter meant to you. I just forgot.' His apology might have stopped the cycle of alienation that anger provokes.

When our actions, even though unintentional, cause harm to others a heartfelt apology is in order. Apologies should not include statements explaining or justifying what we did. When we try to explain how extenuating circumstances caused the mistake, we blunt the force of an apology. People sense that we are diverting blame from ourselves.

Road rage is a strange, new danger on our highways. The Ontario Provincial Police, Canada, receive as many as 500 complaints a week about 'aggressive drivers who wave pistols, shake fists and chase other vehicles at high speeds'.[3]

The problem has become so prevalent on North American highways that one U.S. motorist carries a 'sorry' sign which 'she flashes whenever she inadvertently provokes another driver. "I've found it's very effective in warding off anger," she said. Her insight is borne out by a survey that showed over 85 per cent of road ragers said they would drop the matter if the other "careless" driver simply apologized.'[4]

ILLUSTRATION

Apologies can even save money! A woman who suffered serious burns after scalding herself with a cup of coffee sued the fast-food chain. She offered to settle for $800 and an apology, but the company's chief counsel turned down the offer. She went on to win a judgement in court for several million dollars!

Apologies can defuse volatile and even dangerous situations. While involved in literature evangelism in bazaars in Pakistan I occasionally encountered angry Muslims. They would often bring up the atrocities committed against Muslims by 'Christian' crusaders in the eleventh and twelfth centuries as evidence of the falseness of our faith. When I would express deep regret for the terrible actions of the crusaders, they would usually calm down. Some even became friendly. Then I had a chance to explain the real nature of the Christian faith.

Apologies could do an enormous amount to relieve international tensions. Think what might happen if Palestinians would apologize for terrorist attacks and Israelis for harsh and retaliatory action. Or Serbs for their treatment of Kosovo. Canadian soldiers who suffered under the Japanese in Hong Kong are still waiting for an apology.

Apologies can miraculously resurrect threatened relationships. A brother apologizing to a sister: 'Sis, I'm really sorry about breaking your boom box. I shouldn't have borrowed it. I'll get it repaired or buy you a new one.' A husband apologizing to his wife: 'Honey, I'm sorry about what I said after your accident in the car park. I should have been more worried about you than any damage to the car.'

Why are apologies so hard to give? Probably because they require a certain amount of humility. Our pride fights to maintain the fiction of our superiority. Ego rides again!

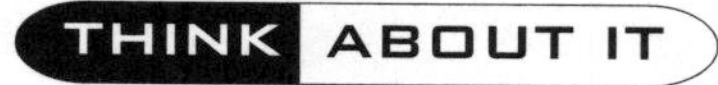

Apologizing to our children!?

In an article on our need to apologize to our children, Geneva Cobb Iijima gives us some good advice on how to apologize:

1. 'Be sincere … speak from the heart.
2. State the offence honestly. For example, 'This morning I broke my promise to…'
3. Express sincere sorrow over the offence… 'I'm very sorry I did that.'
4. Specifically ask for [a response from the person].
5. Don't make excuses… If there are circumstances I must explain, I need to avoid excusing my wrongdoing.
6. Learn from experience.'

Geneva Cobb Iijima, *The Art of Apologizing to Your Children,* Focus on the Family, July 2001, p. 16

Asking for forgiveness and offering an apology are often viewed as interchangeable concepts. Because of the fact that foibles and sins are distinctly different entities, I prefer to distinguish apologies from forgiveness. Human foibles call for forbearance and may entail an apology for unintentional hurt that is caused. Sins call for forgiveness. Let's proceed, then, to define forgiveness.

Defining forgiveness

Based on what we have discussed in previous chapters, we are ready to put together a working definition of forgiveness. Since some aspects remain to be covered in the chapters ahead, this will be an open-ended definition.

1. Forgiveness involves repudiation

Forgiveness begins when we halt the cycle of alienation. Whatever the Holy Spirit uncovers in our heart, whether it be anger, bitterness, resentment, hatred, malice or a desire for vengeance, it must be confessed to God, as the sin it is. Confession without a repudiation of the sin confessed is empty. Repentance follows confession. In this case, repentance means a repudiation of any desire to harm the person who caused the injury.

Gerald Sittser endured months of vengeful thoughts after a terrible accident left his mother, wife and daughter dead. The driver of the other car escaped prosecution due to a technicality. Sittser writes: 'During the months following the trial I thought often about the driver of the other car ... I wanted to see him suffer and pay for the wrong I believed he had done... It eventually occurred to me that this preoccupation was poisoning me. It signaled that I wanted more than justice. I wanted revenge. I was beginning to harbor hatred in my heart. I was edging towards becoming an unforgiving person... The very thought of forgiveness seemed abhorrent to me. I realized at that moment that I had to forgive... Victims can choose life instead of death. They can choose to stop the cycle of destruction and, in the wake of the wrong done, do what is right. Forgiveness is simply choosing to do the right thing.'[5]

2. Forgiveness involves trusting God

When Sittser chose to repudiate hatred and vengeance his healing began. Christians who trust God are able to leave justice in his hands. A repudiation of one's 'natural' desire to see the cause of one's hurt punished is not an act of cowardice, as some cultures might view it, but an act of faith. Sittser continues: 'I think that I was spared excessive preoccupation with revenge because I believe that God is just, even though the judicial system is not. Ultimately every human being will have to stand before God, and God will judge every person with wisdom and impartiality... I also believe that God is merciful, in ways that far exceed what we could imagine or muster ourselves. It is the tension between God's justice and mercy that makes God so capable of dealing with wrong-doers… Forgiving people let God run the universe. They let God punish wrongdoers as he wills, and they let God show mercy as he wills to.'[6]

3. *Forgiveness grows out of humility*

Biblical forgiveness grows out of the honesty about ourselves and others that we considered in chapter two. As we consider the person who has wronged us, we see a person who shares our fallen humanity. In the light of our own tendency to wander, our inclination towards hypocrisy, we have to admit that 'There but for the grace of God go I' — indeed, at other times and in other circumstances we have probably done similarly hurtful things to others. Before we can attempt biblical reconciliation we need a biblical view of our own depravity.

The second part of Lewis Smedes' definition of forgiveness states: 'We must reinterpret the person who wronged us in a larger format… In the act of forgiving, we get a new picture of a needy, weak, complicated, fallible human being like ourselves.'[7] No wonder we are commanded: 'Do nothing out of selfish ambition or vain conceit, but in humility consider others better than yourselves' (Philippians 2:3).

David Augsburger helpfully points out that the root meaning of the English word forgive is give. When we intensify the verb 'we speak of giving at its deepest level, of self-giving, of *giving forth* and *giving up* deeply held parts of the self. To "for-give" is a process of *giving up*. In forgiving we give up demands for perfect behavior, perfect justice, perfect resolution, perfect retribution All we ask is genuine repentance of ourself and of the other. In forgiving we give up the angry picture of the wrongdoer. We put aside the view of the other as an unworthy, unacceptable, unforgivable offender. In forgiving we lay aside the view of ourselves as righteous and the other as totally unrighteous, and we begin to experience the truth that we are both fallible humans in need of being forgiven.'[8]

4. Forgiveness is a gift

Both Ephesians and Colossians command us to forgive as we have been forgiven by God. 'Be kind and compassionate to one another, forgiving each other, just as in Christ, God forgave you' (Ephesians 4:32). 'Forgive as the Lord forgave you' (Colossians 3:13). The forgiveness we have received is an unmerited gift, a gift of grace rooted in God's compassion and sacrificial love. God forgives us in spite of all he knows about our future sins and backslidings.

W. E. Vine defines the Greek word used in these verses, *charizomai,* as 'a favour bestowed unconditionally'.[9] In the disciples' prayer (Matthew 6:12) and in the passage concerning dealing with an unrepentant brother (Matthew 18:21-22) the word *aphiemi* is used. *Aphiemi* has the connotation that a person is freed from sin or that sins are sent forth. In these cases it 'signifies the remission of the punishment due to sinful conduct, the deliverance of the sinner from the penalty Divinely, and therefore, righteously imposed ... such remission is based upon the vicarious and propitiatory sacrifice of Christ. In the O.T., atoning sacrifice and forgiveness are often associated, e.g. Leviticus 4:20, 26.'[10] In these instances repentance and confession are called for in order to have one's sins covered, or forgiven.

In a later chapter we will consider in more detail whether we should withhold forgiveness from the unrepentant. Suffice it to say here that our inability to read the hearts of others makes it very dangerous to withhold forgiveness on the basis of judging the feebleness of another's response — whether or not they sincerely repented. New Testament examples of forgiveness picture it as a lavish, undeserved and unexpected gift. Forgiveness is the gift Jesus gave the woman caught in adultery, the gift he gave Peter after his denials, the gift he gave his crucifiers.

In their study of the subject, Ab-Mabuk, Enright, and Cardis[11] came to the conclusion that 'Forgiveness is an unconditional gift given to one who does not deserve it.'

If forgiveness is a gift, then the recipient must know that it is given. In other words, it must not be kept private, within the heart of the forgiver. It must be offered by the injured party to the one who caused the injury. In secular therapy this might not be essential, since the emotional health of the forgiver is mainly in view. In forgiveness therapy, many practitioners consider it enough if the injured party finds personal freedom from anger and bitterness. In biblical terms, this is not sufficient. Forgiveness must be offered — even if it is not accepted — for it to be genuine.

5. Forgiveness is a gift thankfully given

Since the Christian experiences forgiveness as a gift from God for unimaginable sins, forgiving others for lesser evils ought to come easy. Unfortunately, we often forget the extent of the forgiveness we have received. In chapter three we discussed the redemption we enjoy through the atoning sacrifice of Christ. Hopefully, our reaction is one of profound thankfulness to God.

In the parable to the unforgiving servant Christ warns us about forgetting what God has done for us. You recall the story. In the course of settling accounts, a king discovered that one servant owed him millions of pounds. Since he was unable to pay, the king ordered that his whole family be sold to repay the debt. However, after tearful entreaties the king had pity on him and forgave the whole debt.

When the forgiven servant went out, however, he ran into another servant who owed him a paltry sum. 'He grabbed him and began to choke him. "Pay back what you owe me!" he demanded' (Matthew 18:28). Even though this fellow servant pleaded for patience, the unmerciful servant had him thrown into prison. Grieved by his treatment, other servants told the king. The king called the servant back. '"You wicked servant," he said, "I cancelled all that debt of yours because you begged me to. Shouldn't you have had mercy on your fellow servant just as I had on you?"' (18:32-33).

The king turned the unmerciful servant over to the jailers. Jesus applied this parable by saying, 'This is how my heavenly Father will treat each of you unless you forgive your brother from your heart' (18:35). The lesson is clear. Whenever we approach another, we must colour our perspective with thankfulness for how God has treated us.

6. Forgiveness is a gift given in the process of seeking reconciliation

When we forgive, we engage in a process of seeking to bridge a gulf created by the hurtful actions of another. In his book *The Freedom of Forgiveness*, David Augsburger writes that forgiveness must result in reconciliation.

'Forgiveness is not finally complete until the severed friendship is mended... Authentic forgiveness is the mutual recognition that repentance is genuine and right relationships are achieved. Forgiving requires the grace to accept the other as an equal partner in the search for reconciliation and the genuineness to give repentance or to respond to another's repentance with full trust and respect.'[12]

In a family or church or place of business where a relationship was shattered by actions that ultimately are forgiven, then reconciliation should occur. The quicker the better. This is why not allowing anger to last a night is so important. Since relationships established by God in the body of Christ and in the home are permanent, churches and families should move heaven and earth to effect reconciliation.

However, I would disagree somewhat with Augsburger. We cannot say that forgiveness will restore all relationships. Sometimes there has been no relationship! Forgiving someone who ran into your car does not make him or her a friend — when there was no friendship there in the first place. But it does restore two or more people to a place where a relationship can either develop anew or be restored. This may not take place due to geographic distance or differences of temperament. We cannot force friendships.

It is very unlikely that a woman who forgives the murderer of her friend will establish a relationship with that murderer. However, it is not impossible. In the case of Sydna Massé, whose story I told in an earlier chapter,

Sydna felt constrained to write to Jennie, the murderess. In the course of time, their relationship resulted in Sydna founding a post-abortion programme in two women's prisons![13]

TO SUMMARIZE

Forgiveness is needed for actions that are sinful.

Forbearance is needed where people, for example, make mistakes, have accidents or hold valid opinions concerning which others differ.

Apologies should be offered where unintentional harm has come to someone.

Real forgiveness involves:

1. Repudiating any sin committed or harboured in the heart,
2. Trusting God to take care of justice,
3. Approaching people humbly,
4. Being willing to give or receive forgiveness as a gift,
5. Being thankful for God's undeserved forgiveness,
6. Being willing to be reconciled.

TO SUMMARIZE

Like love, forgiveness is relational. Loving one's neighbour is not something a hermit, in his retreat from others, can experience. Love draws us closer to others. So does forgiveness. It includes a sincere desire for the well-being of the person forgiven. Robert D. Enright believes that 'Forgiveness is one person's heartfelt loving response to another person or people who have hurt the forgiver personally.'[14]

Let's bring these various aspects together into a definition of a forgiving person. *A forgiving person is one who, out of a profound sense of being personally forgiven a great debt by God, is quick to ask forgiveness from another, who repudiates anger, bitterness and a desire for revenge to initiate a loving approach to whoever may have hurt him or her, and who offers to freely forgive and forget the injury caused, with the hope that reconciliation may be achieved.*

QUESTIONS FOR DISCUSSION

1. *Read Romans 14:1-13. Disputes can arise between us for many reasons. In Paul's day some people came into conflict by judging what others ate or by condemning others for keeping certain days special or treating all days alike.*

   a. *What differences of opinion or practice arise today that require forbearance in our dealings with one another?*

DISCUSS IT

b. What do these verses teach about forbearance?
c. How does forbearance differ from forgiveness?

2. *According to Ephesians 4:2 and Colossians 3:12-13 what qualities are essential in one who would live a life of forbearance? Give examples to show how each of these qualities might help us avoid being provoked by another.*

3. *Even when we are at fault, apologizing is often very difficult. Which of the character qualities mentioned in question 2 is most essential if we are to learn to apologize for something we have done? Explain why this is true.*

4. *How does being a thankful person make giving and receiving forgiveness easier?*

5. *Both Ephesians 4:32 and Colossians 3:13 call upon us to forgive as God forgives. Give examples from the life of Jesus Christ that illustrate what this means.*

CHAPTER EIGHT

FORGIVENESS AND RECONCILIATION

LOOK IT UP

BIBLE REFERENCE

'If you are offering your gift at the altar and there remember that your brother has something against you, leave your gift there in front of the altar. First go and be reconciled to your brother; then come and offer your gift' (Matthew 5:23-24).

INTRODUCTION

When she heard that I was writing on forgiveness, one of our friends wrote: 'Let me share a personal experience. I had reason to ask forgiveness of someone who had been upset by some of my bantering remarks that were misunderstood. I failed to recognize that the person concerned was very depressed over family matters. I wrote a brief note of apology since she made it clear she didn't want to see me. She phoned, assuring me of forgiveness and asking me to visit her. I did so, and listened to her describe the many times when something I said had bothered her but she had never expressed it until this last incident. Her last words were to discourage me from visiting her again. (I used to do so frequently.) Is this true forgiveness?'

Our friend asked a very good question. Can forgiveness that does not include a restored relationship be genuine? How can we forgive without making any attempt to reconnect with those estranged from us, be they friends, spouses, siblings, co-workers, neighbours or nations?

Jesus teaches that if a person on the way to worship remembers that someone 'has something against you', he is to immediately 'go and be reconciled to your brother' (Matthew 5:23-24). Apparently, seeking forgiveness is synonymous with seeking reconciliation.

Reconciliation with God

In chapter five we established that alienation was one of the effects of the Fall. Mankind's intimacy with God was the first to suffer. However, the new 'demandingness', to use Larry Crabb's suggestive term, injected conflict into all relationships. God's plan of redemption is aimed at healing those fractures. Among the redeemed, estrangement is to be viewed as an unnatural state.

Certainly, reconciliation with God is intrinsic to salvation. 'Once you were alienated from God and were enemies in your minds because of your evil behaviour. But now he has reconciled you by Christ's physical body through death to present you holy in his sight, without blemish and free from accusation' (Colossians 1:21-22; see also 2 Corinthians 5:18, 20; Romans 5:10).

As believers, the warfare between our rebellious hearts and God's Spirit is over. 'We have peace with God through our Lord Jesus Christ, through whom we have gained access by faith into this grace in which we now stand. And ... God has poured out his love into our hearts by the Holy Spirit, whom he has given us' (Romans 5:1-2, 5). (This is not to deny that our fallen nature will continue to skirmish with our new nature throughout our life.)

The love of God that conquered hate-filled hearts now courses through Spirit-filled arteries — the love that moved God to send his Son to seek estranged sinners. Love transforms us from fighters to peacemakers.

Consider the following astonishing passage. Note the connection between our conversion and our calling. 'Therefore, if anyone is in Christ, he is a new creation; the old has gone, the new has come! All this is from God, who reconciled us to himself through Christ and gave us the ministry of reconciliation: that God was reconciling the world to himself in Christ, not counting men's sins against them. And he has committed to us the message of reconciliation. We are therefore Christ's ambassadors, as though God were making his appeal through us. We implore you on Christ's behalf: Be reconciled to God' (2 Corinthians 5:17-20).

Christ Jesus charges each believer to become an ambassador, commissioned to carry the message of reconciliation to a warring world. This message is centred on the cross where Christ atoned for sin. The passage above reminds us that the transformation of selfish, rebellious sinners by the gospel prepares them to pursue restoration of splintered human relationships.

No wonder the gospel is the hope of the world. It is for this reason that evangelism and missions are the most crucial ministries of the Christian church. (Medical aid, relief and education are wonderful examples of Christian compassion. But they can only relieve surface suffering. They do not alleviate its root cause.) Divorcing couples need the redemptive power of the cross more than they need psychology. The same can be said of fighting teenagers, angry co-workers and warring nations. Without the destruction of sinful 'demandingness', through the operation of the Holy Spirit, what hope is there for restored relationships?

After a powerful movement of the Spirit in a Nebraska town, a woman wrote: 'My husband and I were in the midst of a divorce. He was seeing another woman. Our two daughters were suffering from our sins. My husband and I are both recovering alcoholics and addicts (since 6 years ago) and that's where the devil was heading me again when God saved me through His sinless Son, Jesus Christ. I am guilty of almost every sin known to man ... God has saved my marriage and family and has put a love in my heart and soul more intense than it has ever been. God gave me the power of forgiveness, compassion, understanding, love and control over my weak human will and thoughts. I could not change, no matter how hard I tried. I can do nothing, but with Jesus, anything and everything is possible ... I've been blessed to have committed Christians fighting for me. Whenever I needed help, they were there.'[1]

Since that testimony, the woman's older sister and mother have also been converted. With Christ within, there is hope even for the most splintered of relationships! While the ministry of reconciliation

ILLUSTRATION

refers initially to reconciling people to God, as occurred in this instance, it also leads to the healing of other relationships. This Nebraska marriage was restored.

Restoring human relationships

Learning to live peaceably with others is an important fruit of conversion. 'Make every effort to live in peace with all men' (Hebrews 12:14). 'The wisdom that comes from heaven is first of all pure; then peace-loving, considerate, submissive, full of mercy and good fruit, impartial and sincere' (James 3:17).

In his book *Born Again*, Chuck Colson, President Richard Nixon's convicted 'hatchet man', tells the story of his reconciliation with Senator Harold Hughes. Colson had recently professed faith in Christ when a friend asked Hughes to meet him. Hughes, who stood on the opposite side on many heated issues such as the Vietnam War, responded: 'There isn't anyone I dislike more than Chuck Colson. I'm against everything he stands for.'

After some persuasion, Hughes consented to see Colson. Following dinner at the home of mutual friends, he abruptly asked Colson about his new faith. Impressed by his testimony Hughes immediately forgave Colson, embraced him as a brother and promised to support and defend him. Throughout the bitter Washington Watergate controversy they met regularly for prayer. Hughes stood by him all through his trial and prison term. They became trusted friends.

Often unforgiveness is masked by geographic distance. A person can say over the phone or by letter, 'I forgive you', but since the alienated parties live at some distance, real reconciliation cannot be tested. Ruth Veltkamp, a missionary in Jos, Nigeria, writes that 'There is more than one reason why Fulani are nomads. One of them is to preserve the option of "splitting"... A time-honored Fulani way to settle quarrels [is to] split, move camps in opposite directions, put distance between. Then fighting stops.'[2]

One day Ruth and Nuhu, a Fulani co-worker, became angry with each other. 'I felt he was pushing me when I was already tired. He thought I was being unreasonable. I accused. He was hurt. For two days neither of us made the effort to talk.'

On the third day Nuhu informed her that he had arranged a pick-up truck to move his family to another town. Ruth asked to talk. When they sat down she said, 'I want to ask you to forgive me. What I said the other day I said in anger. Now I can see you had reason to be upset. I'm asking you to forgive me before you move away. I also ask you to pray for me. Especially when I am tired, I am easily tempted to anger.'

Nuhu replied: 'Ever since you spoke those angry words at me, I've had a painful lump in my chest. I cannot live that way. And I did not want to risk that happening again. That is why I said I would move away.

ILLUSTRATION

But since you have asked me to forgive you and pray for you, yes, I will.'

Relieved, Ruth thanked Nuhu and assured him that if it was best for him, he should feel free to move. She writes: 'His answer stunned me. "If I moved now, you would never be sure if I had really forgiven you. I will tell the driver of the pick-up not to come." And that is how I learned what it means to be forgiven — by a nomad. I must say that I have never felt so warmly forgiven before in my life.'

Honest and open confessions of fault, such as that expressed by Ruth to Nuhu, accelerate reconciliation. Often, however, the injured party has to take the initiative if the offending party hangs back. Sometimes it takes years of patient love to restore broken relationships. Jeff Schulte's father forsook his wife and his six children for another woman when Jeff was three. When that relationship soured, he remarried Jeff's mum. Six months later he left for good. In the next twenty years Jeff saw his father twice.

Although Jeff succeeded in sports, in college and in Christian ministry he felt deeply his father's absence. A desire to reconnect led him to journey from Arkansas to Wisconsin to search for him. When they met, instead of chastising his father, Jeff questioned him about his love. 'Of course I love you… Of course I missed you,' his father replied. There was no confession; nor much understanding of the emptiness he had left behind.[3]

Jeff persevered. Probing uncovered the fact that his father was just repeating the scenario of his own youth. 'Jeff decided to love his father with the love of Christ. As he did so, the brittleness between father and son softened. And that softening spread to his siblings, some of whom vowed they could never forgive. But they did.'[4]

Seven years after this initial reunion, all of Jeff's brothers and sisters were reunited with their dad. 'For the first time, Jeff's father broke down and wept. He admitted he had betrayed them and their mother. On the invitation of his children, he moved back to Dayton to be closer to them.' At a golf game later he said, 'I can't believe how all six of you kids have forgiven me. It's unreal.'[5]

Jesus taught: 'Blessed are the peacemakers, for they will be called sons of God' (Matthew 5:9). James wrote: 'Peacemakers who sow in peace raise a harvest of righteousness' (James 3:18). Obviously, bringing injured parties together — as Jeff did — is an important part of our high calling. Ideally, reconciliation should be the initiative of one of the parties to a schism. However, in many cases reconciliation between angry people requires the intervention of someone outside the conflict — a mediator, a peacemaker.

Mediation

Christ is our mediator before the Father. And mediation has historically been an important part of how Christians express their faith. I have been thrust into disputes both here and abroad, controversies between parties that required intervention, usually by a small group of committed Christians. In Pakistan one pastor burned with resentment at the cavalier treatment meted out by another. Two professors vied for positions of power in a seminary. Two brothers in a local church fought incessantly. Marvari believers felt discrimination from Panjabis. In Canada there have been churches disrupted by groups that differed on how the previous pastor was treated, men unable to get along, marriages threatened, families rent by strife.

Mediation is not always successful. I vividly remember an elaborate service of reconciliation held in a Pakistani church. Two brothers expressed forgiveness to each other, hugged each other and promised to get along. On the way out of the service, another missionary overheard one of them saying under his breath, 'I'll forgive him but I'll never set foot in his house again.' He died in this state of alienation.

A mediator will have to talk privately to both parties separately before trying to bring them together. In these sessions he will need to clarify his role, persuade both parties to accept it, establish ground rules and encourage both to tell their stories. Resolution may occur simply as a result of giving antagonists the opportunity to air their views. When light is thrown on grievances, their root can frequently be traced to misunderstandings or insubstantial differences of opinion. They may even seem foolish. After hearing both sides, the mediator will endeavour to get the antagonists to sit down and converse with each other. He will try to clarify issues as they come up. He will apply scriptural principles. While we'll deal with mediation in more detail in the next chapter, it is beyond the scope of this book to handle conflict resolution thoroughly. There are many books written on this subject.[6]

Mediation is not easy. Augsburger writes that 'Grace and truth, acceptance and confrontation, sacrifice and prophetic rebuke are needed in resolving alienation, injustice, or interpersonal injuries.'[7]

Failure to adopt mediation as an option has clogged our courts with litigants. Recognition of this fact has given rise to both Christian and secular models of conflict resolution — a hopeful trend.

Some cultures give a prominent place to mediation. Among the Komonos of the Ivory Coast mediation is a way of life. When missionary Rick Oickle was asked to intercede for a boy with his father, his first thought was to avoid interfering. Oickle writes: 'His father had just beaten his younger brother for refusing to eat and Dauda was next in line. Knowing this he fled from the courtyard. The problem was that their aunt had just fed them and they were too full to eat. Their father thought they were being disobedient. Dauda came to our house and requested that I "beg pardon" of his father. Our houseworker Amara assured me that this was a quite normal request and it didn't matter what the situation was.'[8]

Amara told Rick that he didn't need to explain the whole thing. All he needed to say was: 'Your son came to my place to ask me to come and beg pardon.' When Rick did so the father chuckled and said, 'It's finished. Tell him to come.'

The easy nature of Komono practice, without admission of guilt by the one with the power — the father — raises quite a few questions that missionaries to this tribe will have to address. But at least they accept the importance of a mediator. Not all conflicts can be resolved this easily.

Although reconciliation is the aim in matters of forgiveness, this does not always occur since it depends on the response of the perpetrator of the harm. If the one who caused the initial breach is adamant about refusing to deal with the issues involved, reconciliation will be impossible.

THINK ABOUT IT

THINK ABOUT IT

Rabbi Blumenthal writes: 'Judaism does not recognize *reconciliation* (the whole-hearted yielding of all inner negative feeling) as a necessary part of the process of sin and repentance. Although reconciliation is known and even desirable, rabbinic Judaism realizes that there are other modes of rapprochement that are fully adequate and, perhaps, more realistic.'

David R. Blumenthal, *Repentance and Forgiveness*

Reconciliation is the ideal, but not always the practical option. A mediator might be able to help the friend whose letter I quoted at the beginning of this chapter effect a full restoration of her lost relationship. But then again efforts may be fruitless. She has done what she can. She cannot force her erstwhile friend to restore normal relations. Paul and Barnabas were probably reconciled. (Paul later commends Mark who had been the source of the disagreement.) Still, there is no indication that they resurrected their former one-team approach. Continuing on with separate missionary teams proved to be a wise strategy.

In marriages we should never give up hope of reconciliation. Nevertheless in 1 Corinthians 7 Paul has practical advice for separated couples. The wife who separates, for example, due to abuse, 'must remain unmarried or else be reconciled to her husband' (v. 11). Clearly, a state of separation in extreme circumstances is considered valid.

International reconciliation

What about reconciliation between racial or national enemies? In many places centuries-old hatreds seem ingrained in the ethos of nations. One act of vengeance precipitates retaliation in the escalating spiral of violence that we see played out all over the world. 'During Nazi occupation of the Balkans, Germans and Croats killed hundreds of thousands of Serbs, Gypsies, and Jews... Units of the Croatian Army brazenly flew swastika flags and the old Croatian Fascist symbol.'[9] Before that the Serbs suffered under five centuries of Turkish rule. In the last decade, following the perverted logic of vengeance, Serbs have felt justified to pursue a campaign of 'ethnic cleansing' against Muslims in the Balkans.

Although we view our age as advanced, violence seems to be breaking out — or smouldering just beneath the surface — in places as varied as Zaire, Sudan, China, India, Pakistan, Chechnya, Indonesia, Philippines, Korea, Afghanistan and Columbia, to name a few. This is especially true of the Middle East.

THINK ABOUT IT

In an editorial, Don Posterski lamented the state of Canada. 'For a nation with an international reputation for accommodating our differences and being peacemakers, we are a country rife with hostility.' He sees this in the tensions in our cities, adversarial attitudes between government and labour and especially in the rancour present in parliamentary debate. He urges Canadian Christians to 'live as peacemakers and become instruments of de-escalation'.

Don Posterski, 'A war of verbal hand grenades', *Faith Today*, July-August 1993, p. 13

THINK ABOUT IT

Western democracies are not immune. In the USA at the same time as welfare spending increased by 631%, violent crimes increased by 564%. Neither rising prosperity nor programmes to lift people out of poverty are contributing to a gentler society. The same tendencies have been found all over the world — during the 'enlightened' twentieth century. Wars in the 1900s killed 107.8 million, three times as many as during the whole 400 years between 1500 and 1900, which claimed 34.1 million.[10] The globe seems to be careering out of control.

The message of forgiveness is the only message that can counter this downward spiral into darkness. Theologian Romano Guyardini writes: 'As long as you are tangled in wrong and revenge, blow and counterblow, aggression and defense, you will be constantly drawn into fresh wrong... Only forgiveness frees us from the injustice of others.'[11]

Forgiveness cleanses the human palate of the 'sweet taste of vengeance'. In 1983 two enemies were reconciled in a Belfast jail in Northern Ireland. Both had been involved in the violence and partisan strife that they now renounced. Both were converted in jail. One came from a Protestant background and one from a Roman Catholic home. When asked how they would have responded to each other before their conversion, they 'replied matter-of-factly that they would have attempted to shoot each other'. Liam, the Catholic, had been influenced to change by the faithful visiting of a Protestant mother whose daughter had been shot by a terrorist. She explained her mission: 'Only Christ can heal our troubled land.'[12]

ILLUSTRATION

In his book *What's So Amazing About Grace?* Philip Yancey chronicles how the message of Christian forgiveness, in our time, has produced revolutionary change not only in individuals but also on an international scale. 'In 1989 alone, ten nations — Poland, East Germany, Hungary, Czechoslovakia, Bulgaria, Rumania, Albania, Yugoslavia, Mongolia, the Soviet Union — comprising half a billion people, experienced non-violent revolutions. In many of these, the Christian minority played a crucial role.'[13] Read his fascinating book for concrete examples.

What about those who are the victims of horrific acts of terror? I have had to tear myself away from the TV to write this chapter. The date is September 11, 2001. Images still haunt me weeks later as I review what I have written. A plane smashing into the World Trade Centre in New York. Billows of smoke. Fleeing people. The Pentagon on fire. The collapse of the two towers. Crushed fire-trucks. Mountains of rubble entombing over 3000 people. And now anthrax!

The horror of September 11 makes talk of revenge, retaliation and war seem reasonable and talk of forgiveness obscene. David E. Meadows, a captain in the U.S. Navy, was present in the Pentagon when the horror struck. He wrote:

> Am sitting here having an early morning cup of coffee before I head back to the Pentagon. Our side of the building is

> relatively unharmed, and we have returned to business with a vengeance. The smell of smoke permeates the offices and corridors that are still open and functioning and lingering just along the edges of the smell of smoke is an odor that I would never wish for my children to ever have to endure. The recovering of the bodies continues... I am saddened that we still have many friends and colleagues unaccounted for... We have always known the Pentagon was a target, but the magnitude of the terrorist act against innocent civilians in New York is something we cannot and will not forgive.[14]

Most of the churches that held services on the Sunday following the horror upheld the need to bring the terrorists to justice. Many, however, decried calls for vengeance. This horror, along with infamous abominations such as the Holocaust, the Hutu-Tutsi massacres and Stalin's purges are too horrific to comprehend. Professor Robert K. Rudolph used to remind us that trying to understand the reason for evil is like trying to find a rationale for irrationality. Evil on this magnitude is beyond comprehension.

Public safety in the entire world will require a concerted effort to root out terrorism. The Christian should have no problem with this call to take up arms against evil. The biblical peacemaker is not a pacifist. But without some approach to alienated nations can we ever hope to be free of terrorism? Without meeting, talking, listening to grievances — without seeking to understand the fears and frustrations of other peoples, we are doomed to keep on feeding the fires of chaos.

Can we even conceive of forgiving the evil men who brought this disaster on innocent people? That will be hard; very hard. And yet we know that there is no sin that is so great that God will not forgive a repentant sinner. The soldier who oversaw Jesus' crucifixion was forgiven. Some of the Pharisees who engineered Jesus' death became his disciples. Simon, the Jewish terrorist, became one of the twelve. Murderers such as Moses and David were forgiven. If God is so merciful, who are we to drag our feet?

Wherever we live, wherever we serve, we must act. Why? King Jesus is the Prince of Peace. We are his ambassadors. That may mean being reconciled with a brother or sister, parent or uncle. It may mean being reconciled with a coworker or neighbour. It may mean we will need to step in and mediate disputes in our families, our churches, our schools, our businesses and our communities. Some of us may be called to mediate peace between peoples. Whenever antagonists embrace, the angels sing.

QUESTIONS FOR DISCUSSION

1. Read 2 Corinthians 5:17-21.

a. Why do we need to be reconciled to God?

b. *On what basis is God able to reconcile us to himself?*
c. *Why is this only possible when we are made new?*
d. *Once reconciled to God, what ministry do we receive?*

2. *Read Matthew 5:9. What is a peacemaker?*

3. *Re-read James 4:1-3. In an earlier chapter we discussed how blocked goals create anger. Anger, in turn, often leads to alienation and conflict.*
   a. *According to these verses what do the blocked goals usually represent?*
   b. *How might isolating the blocked goals or desires of two parties help lay the groundwork for reconciliation?*

4. *Read Philippians 4:2-3. If you were their friend, what would you do to reconcile Euodia and Syntyche?*

5. *Read 1 Corinthians 6:1-6.*
   a. *What would you do if you were in leadership of a church where two members have a serious dispute?*
   b. *(Optional) What should be done if a husband and wife are so at odds that they seek divorce?*

6. *Read Hebrews 12:14. Give some examples where reconciliation might not work out. What is there that makes it easier to reconcile Christians with each other?*

7. *(Optional.) Consider a current area of conflict in the world. If you were in a position to reduce tension in that situation, what might you do?*

Part Two

PRACTICAL QUESTIONS ABOUT FORGIVENESS

CHAPTER NINE

WHO TAKES THE FIRST STEP?

LOOK IT UP

BIBLE REFERENCE

'If your brother sins against you, go and show him his fault, just between the two of you. If he listens to you, you have won your brother over' (Matthew 18:15).

INTRODUCTION

Resentment shreds the fabric of human relationships from the bedrooms of suburbia to the corridors of power. Bitterness smoulders among the rags. The hurts are so painful. What do we do? We know we should do something, but we look sideways, waiting for the other person to make the first move. Wasn't he the cause? Aren't we the offended party?

The innocent party

Many put off reconciliation while they wait for the more guilty party to initiate dialogue. The person most responsible for the grievance, however, may not even recognize that an offence has been committed, or may not be willing to take the initiative. Furthermore, it is often impossible to apportion blame accurately, since any disagreement has two sides.

Even if I am the one going around with the proverbial dagger in my back, Christ expects from me a revolutionary response. 'If your brother sins against you, go and show him his fault, just between the two of you' (Matthew 18:15-17). There it is in black and white. Although I might be the innocent victim of a brother's sin, Jesus asks me to take the first step towards reconciliation. But what about the guilty party? Has he no responsibility to seek reconciliation?

The guilty party

Ideally, the one who sins should be the one who makes the first move. Christ taught that if a person on the way to worship remembers that another has a grievance against him (due to something he has said or done) he should stop what he is doing, seek out the offended party and apologize with an eye to reconciliation (Matthew 5:23-24).

These instructions assume that a breach in fellowship can be traced to a real transgression — we've already talked about dealing with imagined offences in chapter seven. Human foibles, mistakes and accidents call for forbearance not forgiveness. But without taking the effort to talk about the issues behind a severed fellowship, one of the parties may classify the cause to be sin. Even if it is not sin, the one whose mistake led to the alienation should offer a sincere apology.

Suppose the cause is a real, not imagined, transgression. When I have sinned against a brother or sister, I must come to them humbly, asking for forgiveness for my sin. I must call a spade, a spade — not try to alleviate

ILLUSTRATION

my guilt by voicing excuses. Not, 'I'm really sorry for lashing out at you but the way you spoke made me think you were criticizing my work.' Or, 'I'm sorry I swore at you, but your car came too close.' Or, 'I just wasn't myself.'

Nor does dealing with conflict in a loving way mean that we hide sinful behaviour under a blanket of fuzzy verbiage. 'I apologize if I've done anything wrong (even though I can't think of anything).' Christ commands us to be clear and accurate about admitting sin and facing faults: 'I'm sorry I lost my temper'; 'Forgive me for questioning your motives'; 'Forgive me for calling you stupid'; 'I'm sorry for falsifying the story I told the elders about you. It was really wrong.'

Pat's mother, Mrs Denson, had always had problems with violence. When Pat was converted her animosity intensified. One day, on her way out to a youth rally, her mother snatched her Bible, threw it across the room, grabbed her by the hair and knocked her head on the floor again and again. She shouted at her not to ever talk to her about God again.

Waking up in a hospital room after a long period of unconsciousness, Pat explained to her doctor what had happened. A day or so later she woke to see her mother pacing back and forth outside. Although fearful, she prayed for protection. The nurse assured her that the police had issued a restraining order. Quoting a verse she had memorized brought peace to her heart and she slept again. But when she awoke her mother was straightening the sheets. She flinched when her mother reached out to touch her.

Her mum began to cry. 'Pat, I'm so sorry for what I've done. I hate myself for hurting you. I've been here all night trying to find a way to make things right. Please, forgive me. I need your forgiveness. I even need God's forgiveness.'

Feelings of pain, fear and anger surged through Pat — then a sense of peace and love enabled her to stretch out her hand and touch her mother's forehead. 'Mum, I love you, and I forgive you. The Lord loves you even more. He wants to forgive all your sins. He suffered more for you than I have.'

Mrs Denson asked Pat to tell her about God's forgiveness. Before long she prayed with her daughter, asking the Lord for forgiveness. Later, when police took her away, she assured her daughter that she would get help for her temper.[1]

Third party — a peacemaker

If both the offender and the one offended stall the process, a third party may need to step in. Consider a passage in Galatians: 'Brothers, if someone is caught in a sin, you who are spiritual should restore him gently. But watch yourself, or you also may be tempted. Carry each other's burdens, and in this way you will fulfil the law of Christ. If anyone thinks he is something when he is nothing, he deceives himself' (Galatians 6:1-3).

Note firstly that observing a believer caught in a sin carries with it a responsibility to try and restore that fallen person. Why? Because, contrary to social mores which decree 'I am not my brother's keeper', the law of Christ declares that we are to 'bear each other's burdens'. The law of Christ is the law of love. 'A new command I give you: Love one another. As I have loved you, so you must love one another. By this all men will know that you are my disciples, if you love one another' (John 13:34-35). Since we are part of one family, members of one body, we can never say, 'Oh, that's not my responsibility.'

Note secondly that, since restoration should be attempted with great care, it needs to be carried out by those 'who are spiritual', that is, mature in Christ. Restoring a fallen brother often leads to volatile emotions. An angry response from a fallen Christian may provoke an unprepared peacemaker to become personally angry or to blurt out hurtful words which will make matters worse. Great tact is needed lest we pour fuel on a smouldering relational fire or ignite tensions where none existed. Since the reconciler needs to lay bare the murkiness of the sin involved, he must come equipped with the ability to discern between sin and human foibles, as discussed in chapter seven. Patience too must be brought to bear since timing is crucial if we are to avoid being charged with meddling.

Of course, this does not absolve an immature Christian from attempting to privately restore those who are in their immediate family or circle of friends. The procedure described by Christ in Matthew 18 makes every Christian responsible. (We will consider that in the next chapter.)

Nevertheless, these verses in Galatians do warn us to use great care when the law of Christ calls us to step into a third-party dispute or to restore a fallen Christian. Mature Christians, including church leaders, should shoulder the primary responsibility.

Note, thirdly, that restoration should be attempted humbly and gently. The mediator will probably be tempted to feel very superior to the sinning brother. As we saw in an earlier chapter, a sense of our own fallibility and fallenness is indispensable when dealing with forgiveness. Self-righteousness disqualifies us. It also clouds our judgement.

Clarifying the transgression involved is crucial. Unfortunately, we often react too hastily to perceived sins in others. Almost without thinking we elevate ourselves to a place of judgement. But our perceptions are often the result of misunderstandings or prejudices. We tend to stereotype others by putting them into categories. Human relationships are seldom so clear-cut. What we perceive as sin may be nothing more than a human failing. No wonder Jesus commanded: 'Do not judge, or you too will be judged… Why do you look at the speck of sawdust in your brother's eye and pay no

ILLUSTRATION

attention to the plank in your own eye?' (Matthew 7:1, 3).

In his inimitable way, Eddie Askew takes these words of Christ and encapsulates them in verse:

Lord, the only one I'm slow to judge is me.
Where I'm concerned
I always see the extenuating circumstances.
And find it easy to forgive.
But turn it around,
put others in the dock,
and I bring in a verdict without hesitation.
Guilty and with no appeal.

It's all so easy, Lord,
to find a reason to condemn.
To criticise, hold up another's faults.
Makes me feel good.
Helps me to hide the truth
of my own weaknesses
behind a mask, empty.
Fragile as tissue, Lord,
thin as skin and yet persistent.
I see it all in black and white.
At one end or the other of the scale.
...
Help me to look with eyes of love,
like yours.[2]

(extract from No Strange Land*; published with permission of Leprosy Mission International)*

William Barclay gave three reasons why judging another can cause so many problems.

1. We never know the whole facts or the whole person. We cannot understand the circumstances or temptations.
2. It is almost impossible for anyone to be strictly impartial in judgement.
3. No one is good enough to judge another. Our own faults and our own inability to resolve them automatically disqualify us as fair critics.[3]

While what Barclay says is true, there is another danger here. Reasoning such as this holds many Christians back from ever saying anything critical of another — even if sins as obvious as gossip or adultery are involved. People excuse themselves by saying, 'Who am I to judge?' If we never make a moral judgement, however, we will condemn ourselves to wallowing in a 'See no evil. Hear no evil' swamp.

The Bible not only commands us not to judge, but it also commands us to discern. Paul queries: 'Is it possible that there is nobody among you wise enough to judge a dispute between believers?' (1 Corinthians 6:5). 'Test everything. Hold on to the good' (1 Thessalonians 5:21). 'But among you there must not be even a hint of sexual immorality, or of any kind of impurity, or of greed, because these are improper for God's holy people' (Ephesians 5:3). Although striking a balance between sinful tolerance and sinful judgement is very difficult, it must be done.

TO SUMMARIZE

TO SUMMARIZE

Wherever sins or misunderstandings create breaches in human relationships, someone needs to step forward to initiate reconciliation. The Bible gives us a clear mandate for:

1. The innocent person to go to the one who has sinned and offer forgiveness and reconciliation;
2. The one who has sinned to make the first move by seeking forgiveness from those harmed;
3. A third party, a peacemaker, to carefully seek to reconcile those alienated — where both the offender and the one offended stall the process.

Like peacekeepers in Bosnia who negotiate minefields in the fulfilment of their duties, Christian peacemakers attempt a work fraught with dangers. While ultimate judgement must be left to God who alone is impartial and omniscient, the New Testament calls us to lovingly discern the acts of others. Perhaps the difference between biblical discernment and self-righteous judgement is a difference of attitude. Do we look down on those we judge, or do we look at them through eyes of understanding and love? Compassion requires us to climb down off our judgement seat.

To do that we'll need lots of humility and the patience to listen.

Like good conversation, forgiveness requires good listeners. The one who takes the initiative in pursuing reconciliation needs to listen very carefully to how others describe a situation, whether that person be the innocent party, the guilty party or a third party. 'Every one should be quick to listen, slow to speak and slow to become angry' (James 1:19). Too much anger is rooted in misunderstandings. Misunderstandings develop when we do not listen, when we interrupt others in the middle of an explanation, when we finish their sentences for them, when we stop listening in a conversation to plan our next verbal gambit, when we try to read between the lines. Attentive listeners who control their tongue gain insights that inhibit outbursts of anger.

THINK ABOUT IT

> To love is to listen. Those who listen to others are saying, non-verbally, 'I think you're important. I want to hear what you have to say. I want to understand your side of the story.'

Listening will help us gain some inkling into the feelings, motives and even prejudices of others. We should avoid coming to a conclusion too quickly. It is better to repeat the key points made and ask the person if our summary is correct. Beverly Smith suggests that we 'Ask for more information. Say things like, "And then what happened?" or "What did you do then?" or "How did you feel about that?" If the speaker jumps from one subject to another or hasn't really thought about how he feels, suggest, "Let's go back a minute to the time that..."'[4]

Although our goal is to understand the person and the situation, we must remind ourselves that complete understanding is impossible to attain. Augsburger writes: 'Perfect understanding of any other person might breed contempt, not forgiveness. Any human understanding of another human is tainted with our own evil. None of us is good enough to be entrusted with complete knowledge of another. That's impossible to begin with... Where we cannot understand, it is still possible to be understanding... In being understanding we accept the complexity of human motivation, the contradictions in persons that are beyond our explanation. We realize that there are ambivalences and inner tensions we will not be able to explain, but we can embrace in the arms of understanding, complex and terrifying as they often are.'[5]

Being understanding! Paul urges the Corinthians to realize the difference between 'having knowledge' and 'being understanding'. 'If I ... can fathom all mysteries and all knowledge ... but have not love, I am nothing' (1 Corinthians 13:2). Samuel Lopez De Victoria, pastor of Miami Grace Church, captures this contrast in a piece he wrote entitled, 'I'm So Sorry'. Let me quote several verses:

> I am so sorry that I did not understand your pain.
> Walking through fire has opened my eyes.
>
> ...
>
> I am so sorry that I hit you with God talk making
> you feel unspiritual.
> I misused God's sword and hurt you
> instead of being an agent of release and healing.
>
> ...
>
> I am so sorry that I did not pay the price to enter
> your world
> but blindly insisted mine as the only valid one.
> I have much to learn and appreciate.
>
> ...
>
> I am so sorry that I recklessly assumed you had a
> bad attitude.
> I was masking my insecurities.
>
> ...
>
> I am so sorry that I did not extend to you the same
> mercy
> and grace God has to me. Amazing grace I have
> not shared.
>
> ...
>
> Please pray for me and if you find it in your heart
> to have mercy on me,
> a poor wretched soul ... then I beg of you
> to please forgive me.[6]

We must not wait until friendships lie in charred ruins at our feet before we pursue reconciliation. Whether we are the cause, the victim or a third party, we cannot afford to look the other way. You! I! Whoever we are, we must take the first step!

Among Christians this is the duty of love, a duty that calls for understanding born of an empathetic awareness of our shared humanity and a commitment to listen patiently to the parties in a dispute.

As we listen we may discover that the sin was no sin at all, but the result of a human foible, a mistake, an accident, a misunderstanding. If so, forbearance, as considered in chapter seven, is the salve we need to apply to the damaged relationship.

When forgiveness is offered and received, the very trees of the field sing for joy. A daughter is reconciled to her father. A husband and wife embrace. Friends smile again. Enemies begin to talk. Church splits heal. The sun shines brighter. Satan flees. God is in his heaven and life is good. And with the anger gone — we can sleep! As spring breaks out all around us we ask ourselves why this took us so long.

QUESTIONS FOR DISCUSSION

It is natural for us to use apparently legitimate excuses to avoid the difficult task of seeking to reconcile two parties in a conflict, or to ask for or give forgiveness. Answer each of the excuses below using the verses provided, or others of your own choice.

1. *'It's none of my business.' How does Philippians 2:3-5 nullify this excuse?*

2. *'I can never understand why he/she did/said that.' Understanding develops when we follow the advice of James 1:19 and develop a crucial skill.*

    a. *Name a time during the last week or so when you failed to really listen to someone.*
    b. *Think back over the week and write down something new you learned about someone as a result of really listening to them.*
    c. *Explain why listening is so important when seeking to resolve alienation.*

3. *'Something should be done about this situation, but someone else should make the first move.' Who is asked to make the first move in each of the verses below?*

    a. *1 John 1:9*
    b. *Matthew 5:23-24*
    c. *Matthew 18:15*
    d. *Galatians 6:1-2*

4. *'It's not my business to judge him or her. Didn't Jesus say, "Judge not that you be not judged"?' If we are just*

DISCUSS IT

to overlook the sins of others, and expect others to overlook our sins, then we don't need to be concerned about forgiveness and reconciliation. Reconcile the apparent conflict between the following verses: Matthew 7:1, 3; 1 Corinthians 6:2, 5; 1 Thessalonians 5:21; Hebrews 5:14.

5. *Draw up a short summary statement about who is responsible for initiating reconciliation or seeking forgiveness where sin creates alienation.*

CHAPTER TEN

HOW DO CONGREGATIONAL AND INDIVIDUAL APPROACHES DIFFER?

LOOK IT UP

BIBLE REFERENCE

'Brothers, if someone is caught in a sin, you who are spiritual should restore him gently. But watch yourself, or you also may be tempted. Carry each other's burdens, and in this way you will fulfil the law of Christ' (Galatians 6:1-2).

INTRODUCTION

Is there a difference between how a congregation deals with offences and how individuals should handle forgiveness? Yes, there is.

When Ben left his wife to move in with the choir director, their church was thrown into turmoil. Repeated attempts to urge Ben to return to his wife were rebuffed. In a sombre business meeting, the pastor tearfully recommended that Ben and his mistress, Gwendeline, be struck from the membership list. Some agreed. A vocal minority urged the congregation to exercise compassion by giving them more time to repent. Others responded that by delaying action they were confirming them in their sin. Some felt that the crisis had been caused by a lowering of the standards. They worried openly about the effect this may have among the young people. Eventually, a vote was taken and both were removed from membership. A visit was to be scheduled and a letter sent to explain the church's action and to inform them that the door of repentance was always open.

THINK ABOUT IT

Individual Christians are called to demonstrate revolutionary grace. Churches must display the same radical grace, but — at times — this has to be balanced by actions of apparent severity. Otherwise the moral testimony of the church will be compromised.

Failure to distinguish between our responsibilities as individuals and the duties of a local church body creates confusion. This confusion, in turn, damages the church's moral climate by hampering its ability to deal decisively with sin. Without decisive action the church's light grows dim. While balancing personal and congregational responsibilities can often seem like walking across the Niagara Gorge on a tightrope, it must be undertaken.

Let me illustrate this distinction on several levels. God has delegated responsibility to uphold justice in society to human governments. We expect our policemen to enforce the law. But we brand as vigilantes citizens who take the law into their own hands. We depend on our courts, not individuals, to mete out justice. The same crime calls for differing actions depending on whether one is an agent of government or a private citizen. A private citizen, certainly a Christian citizen, must never undertake vengeful actions. And yet concerning civil authority we read: 'The authorities that exist have been established by God… He [the ruler] does not bear the sword for nothing. He is

God's servant, an agent of wrath to bring punishment on the wrongdoer' (Romans 13:1, 4).

Ruling authorities in a democracy — the parliament and the justice system — receive from God the authority to administer punishments, including the death penalty (the sword). In time they will be called to give account to God for their stewardship of justice and mercy. You may very well differ with me here. But I believe that to flounder here is to dissipate present deterrence and damage future generations. Compromise on this issue injects chaos into society by failing to hold people accountable for evil acts. When a society fails to demonstrate that such acts have consequences they mortgage long-term compassion and tranquillity for short-term sentimentality.

Consider a second example, the matter of war, where a larger community must do what an individual must not. Here is another topic concerning which Christians sincerely differ. In my opinion, a country must protect its citizens from attack and engage in just wars. On the other hand, in our day-to-day relationships, when someone 'smites us on one cheek' we are to 'turn the other cheek'.

The distinction between corporal and individual approaches to forgiveness reflects these paradoxes. On a personal level we need to show an openness to extend unlimited forgiveness. On a church level, Christ commands us to discipline the unrepentant, with a view to their restoration, by treating them 'as you would a pagan or a tax collector' (Matthew 18:17). I'm very puzzled that some of the main books I read while doing research on forgiveness failed to make this distinction.

This distinction is hard to maintain in our hyper-individualistic societies. We have soaked up so much emphasis on 'my rights' and 'my freedoms' that we have little concept of 'my responsibilities' to family, neighbourhood, community or even nation. When we accept the Christian faith, however, we accept its corporate implications. God calls us into his family. We become part of the body of Christ. We join a local church. The Holy Spirit moves us to be concerned about the unreached of the world, about widows, orphans, refugees, prisoners — and each other. The 'me, myself and I' mentality is replaced by a 'love your neighbour' attitude.

Biblical teaching about church discipline assumes a commitment to the church community. Without such a commitment, restoration will be difficult or impossible. In the mid-80s Pastor Gordon MacDonald committed adultery, confessed his sin and was brought under eighteen months of church discipline. Neither the discipline necessary nor his subsequent restoration would have been possible without his commitment to the church and their commitment to him.

Today Gordon MacDonald celebrates restorative grace as 'one of the church's greatest ministries'. In an interview in Montreal by Timothy Ernst, MacDonald emphasized the importance of the church as a body.

EXPLANATION

'Evangelical Christianity is scandalously individualistic... As believers we haven't adequately appreciated that the Bible is a relational book. Biblical culture knew nothing of the kind of individualism we foster today. People then were tightly interlocked in families and communities. There was a deep consciousness of their forefathers and their children. Nehemiah confessed the sins of his father; Job prayed for the sins of his children ... Aaron and Hur stood beside Moses holding his arms high so his prayers would be effective... They were a team. Similarly, God has called us to relationships today... There's a biblical concept of protecting, developing, rebuking and rejoicing with one another... If the church believes in repentance, it must provide a caring fellowship in which it is safe to repent.'[1]

Dealing with those who fall is never easy — but if we can develop a caring fellowship, we can minimize the anguish. That means we must follow the example of Christ. 'Be completely humble and gentle; be patient, bearing with one another in love' (Ephesians 4:2). 'Make my joy complete by being like-minded, having the same love, being one in spirit and purpose. Do nothing out of selfish ambition or vain conceit, but in humility consider others better than yourselves. Each of you should look not only to your own interests, but also to the interests of others. Your attitude should be the same as that of Christ Jesus' (Philippians 2:2-5).

Projecting an attitude of love and compassion towards others should not be that difficult. After all, that which brings us together in any genuine local church is not only our faith in Jesus Christ but our shared experience of his grace. We are not theologians gathered together to debate weighty issues — although we may do that from time to time. No, we are wounded, forgiven sinners taking the cure. 'If we claim to be without sin, we deceive ourselves and the truth is not in us' (1 John 1:8). When we see the church — our church — as a hospital for sinners, the conceit and self-righteousness that make restoring a fallen brother impossible dissipates. When all members share this humble realization the church becomes open to hear confession and accept repentance.

No matter how much property our church has, no matter how long a history, no matter how much stained glass or how many people attend — it is a congregation of forgiven sinners or it has no right to be called a church. Ron Davis reminds us that the church is 'the fellowship of the forgiven! God calls us to receive His free-flowing forgiveness, and to turn around and pour that same forgiveness out on everyone around us — liberally, lavishly, exuberantly — in gratitude to God for the abundant, extravagant, unconditional love and forgiveness he has given us!'[2] While we might add an emphasis on repentance and 'tough love', we cannot fault the spirit in which Davis makes his point.

Developing a forgiving fellowship is not easy. Maintaining it is even more difficult. We are exhorted: 'Make every effort to keep the unity of the Spirit through the bond of peace. There is one body and one Spirit — just as you were called to one hope when you were called — one Lord, one faith, one baptism; one God and Father of all, who is over all and through all and in all' (Ephesians 4:3-6). Our unity is not based on some emotional attachment to others. It is based upon the spiritual union of believers through the Holy Spirit with each other, with Christ as Lord and with the Father. It is also based upon a shared confession of one faith, one hope and one spiritual baptism into Christ. Our unity is not organizational. It is of the spirit. But to demonstrate this practically and publicly requires all members to 'make every effort to keep the unity'.

How is that unity threatened? A caring fellowship is a fragile flower. When the integrity of that fellowship is compromised by the actions of one member, the body must take action. That action, though compassionate, must be decisive and disciplinary. 'You must not associate with anyone who calls himself a brother but is sexually immoral or greedy, an idolater or a slanderer, a drunkard or a swindler. With such a man do not even eat' (1 Corinthians 5:11). The Scripture requires us to take disciplinary action in at least the following cases:

- Immorality (1 Corinthians 5:1-5, 9, 11)
- Behaviour that creates conflicts and divisions

(Titus 3:9-11). 'Warn a divisive man once, and then warn him a second time. After that, have nothing to do with him.'

- Dishonesty — stealing, lying, swindling (1 Corinthians 5:11)
- Materialism or greed (1 Corinthians 5:11)
- Slander, backbiting, gossip (1 Corinthians 5:11)
- False teaching (2 John 10-11; 1 Timothy 1:19-20)
- False religions — idolatry (1 Corinthians 5:11; Titus 1:10-14)
- Laziness (2 Thessalonians 3:6-15)
- Addiction (1 Corinthians 5:11)

THINK ABOUT IT

Church discipline in the *Westminster Confession*

'Church censures (discipline) are necessary, for the reclaiming and gaining of offending brethren, for deterring others from like offences, for purging out of the leaven which might infect the whole lump, for vindicating the honour of Christ, and the holy profession of the Gospel, and for preventing the wrath of God, which might justly fall upon the Church, if they should suffer His covenant, and the seals thereof, to be profaned by notorious and obstinate offenders.'

Westminster Confession, Chapter XXX, Part IV

Church discipline protects the church. To use the imagery of our Master, sin is a leaven that can decimate a whole congregation. Immorality compromises its purity. Divisiveness and slander shatter its unity and love. False teaching removes the heart of the very faith upon which it rests.

The Westminster Assembly viewed discipline as fulfilling five functions: restoring offending brethren, deterring others, protecting the church from the effects of sin, maintaining the church's testimony to Christ and the gospel, and preventing sterner discipline from God from falling on the church.

How then are we to proceed in the case of a fallen member? In Matthew 18, Christ outlines the four-step approach a congregation is to take. 'If your brother sins against you, go and show him his fault, just between the two of you. If he listens to you, you have won your brother over. But if he will not listen, take one or two others along, so that every matter may be established by the testimony of two or three witnesses. If he refuses to listen to them, tell it to the church; and if he refuses to listen even to the church, treat him as you would a pagan or a tax collector' (vv. 15-17).

Step One: The person immediately concerned in the breach privately approaches the brother at fault with a view to being reconciled with him. The vast majority of offences occur privately, between people in a relationship: a husband and wife, two friends, two co-workers, brothers and sisters. Hence most offences should be addressed at this level by those personally involved. By handling a fault confidentially, the danger of creating gossip or injecting division into a church can be avoided.

The person who takes this first step towards restoring the sinning brother will require tact, humility and compassion. He will need to listen patiently to the offending brother's side of the offence. As we've already seen from Galatians 6, he should approach the person gently, but firmly. Declaration of the sin involved must not be avoided or sugar-coated. If the person responds with confession, sorrow and evident repentance, gentleness will prevail. Should the fallen brother justify his sin, plead extenuating circumstances or angrily reject the reconciler's entreaty the latter will be compelled to move from a gentle appeal to a rebuke and from rebuke to censure. Continued refusal to admit fault leads to step two.

Step Two: When initial efforts are rebuffed, then one or two more should join the first person in an effort to lead the offender to repentance. The same guidelines apply throughout this procedure: gentleness, clarity, firmness, patient listening. The passage in Galatians 6 (v. 1) points out that restoration should be attempted by mature Christians who have experience in avoiding the temptation to become angry, self-righteous or careless with their tongue. If there are mature Christians within the circle of the two parties to this offence, then they should be asked to participate. In serious cases, church leaders (elders, deacons) will be the ones chosen to go to the recalcitrant offender. One visit is seldom enough. If there are signs that the offending brother is sensitive to their appeal, the matter should not be rushed. Confidentiality should still be maintained at all cost.

Sometimes a group of people will take up the case of the offending brother in opposition to those who would rebuke him. This can lead to conflict in a church. For this reason, many have wisely suggested that the pastor should not be among those who seek to restore the brother. The pastor will probably have been consulted privately by the offended party and suggested the steps that should be taken. By staying impartial at this stage, the pastor can maintain objectivity. He remains the shepherd of the whole flock. Of course, if the conflict spreads to others beyond those immediately involved, then the next step should be taken.

Step Three: If the sinning brother remains adamantly unrepentant, the matter needs to be brought to the whole church. The offending person will be informed of this step in advance. Even here, confidentiality needs to be stressed. The matter will first be discussed by the church leadership. Then it will be taken to a church meeting, restricted to the actual members of the church. At this meeting appropriate Scripture will need to be presented, since many members may have little experience with church discipline. The sin will be stated clearly. The congregation will be urged to pray earnestly for the repentance of the offender. Those who have a relationship with the person may be encouraged to appeal for his repentance.

Step Four: If the sinning brother rejects the urging of the whole church, discipline will be required. That discipline may take milder or more severe forms depending on the nature of the offence and the stubbornness of the person. At the very least, the person will be required to resign from church offices and responsibilities for a duration. The *Westminster Confession* outlines this progression of steps: 'For better attaining these ends (e.g. restoration and vindication of gospel) the officers of the Church are to proceed by admonition, suspension from the sacrament of the Lord's Supper for a season; and by excommunication from the Church according to the nature of the crime, and the demerit of the person.'[3]

The aim is always the restoration of the person — 'to win the brother'. If forbidding the person to take communion for an interval accomplishes this result, so much the better. If not, severer measures will include excommunication, being dropped from the church membership role. This will mean that the person is advised that he is not welcome to attend church meetings and fellowships. Agonizing as it may seem, cutting this person off from fellowship may have a positive result.

TO SUMMARIZE

Biblical texts list immorality, idolatry, divisiveness, dishonesty, greed, slander, false teaching, laziness and addiction among those sins that require disciplinary action by a local church.

Matthew 18:15-17 outlines four steps in the five-step process of church discipline.

1. The confidential attempt by the person most immediately affected by the breach to lead the person at fault to repentance and restoration.
2. When the individual is rejected, he or she is to secure one or two more to help in attempting restoration while maintaining confidentiality.
3. Bringing the matter to the whole church if the person at fault remains adamantly unrepentant.
4. Upon rejection of the church's urging, the unrepentant sinner is to be disciplined.

TO SUMMARIZE

Step Five: The goal of church discipline must always be restoration to fellowship. Paul described the discipline of the immoral man in Corinth as handing 'this man over to Satan, so that the sinful nature may be destroyed and his spirit saved on the day of the Lord' (1 Corinthians 5:5). The man in question had committed fornication with his father's wife. In his case discipline did result in restoration. Evidently, the agony of soul produced in the person by being cut off from family and friends moved him to repentance. Paul had to urge the Corinthians in a second letter to forgive this man. 'The punishment inflicted on him by the majority is sufficient for him. Now instead, you ought to forgive and comfort him, so that he will not be overwhelmed by excessive sorrow. I urge you, therefore, to reaffirm your love for him ... in order that Satan might not outwit us. For we are not unaware of his schemes' (2 Corinthians 2:6-8, 11). Undue delay in forgiving a person who has shown signs of repentance gives the devil an opportunity to insinuate that the church is a harsh, legalistic, unloving place.

In this regard we need to remember that there is no sin, not even murder, that cannot be forgiven. Remember David and Paul? Actually, the only iniquity that cannot be forgiven is impenitence — refusal to repent.

How do we discern the quality of a person's repentance? What is involved in readmitting an excommunicated person to membership or allowing him to again take up church duties? This is not easy. Recently a friend described how an adulterer was welcomed back in an emotional service at a church he visited.

EXPLANATION

Unfortunately, a few weeks later the man again left his wife to move in with his lover! Apparently, the pastor and leadership had felt that the man's verbal expression of repentance was enough to warrant immediate reinstatement. Was the injured wife consulted about his sincerity? Or was this all undertaken beneath a fuzzy understanding of grace?

Clearly, testing the sincerity of a person's repentance requires the elapse of some time. But how do we avoid both foolish naïveté and harsh gracelessness? Seeking a balance is notoriously difficult. Consider the practice of the early church.

During the first two hundred years the church was very strict about granting restoration to those who sinned after baptism. 'Thinkest thou that the sins of those who repent are straightway remitted? By no means; but he who repenteth must vex his soul, and humble himself mightily in all his conduct ... and if he bear the afflictions that come upon him, He who created and empowered all things shall certainly be moved to compassion and give him healing.'[4] The early church had a ceremony of absolution to formally restore the offender. For three postbaptismal sins, however, forgiveness was left to God alone.

Controversy arose in the early years of the third century when Callistus, upon becoming Bishop of Rome, began to grant absolution more quickly. He felt that current church practice discouraged repentance. Others in the church opposed his stand. In A. D. 250 the Emperor Decius launched a full-scale persecution aimed at producing apostates, not martyrs. Under pressure, many believers denied the faith. Following his death, the church faced the dilemma of what to do with these apostates who sought re-entry into the church.

Cyprian, Bishop of Carthage, wrote a treatise, *The Lapsed*, to deal with the problem. He felt that if restoration was granted by simply saying, 'I'm sorry', why would anyone stay true during subsequent persecutions? Eventually he decided that the lapsed could be readmitted only after proving their sincerity. He advocated:

1. Public confession of the sin;
2. Demonstrated contrition for a period of time;
3. Restoration by laying on of hands;
4. Restriction from official leadership roles for those who had been church leaders.[5]

Surely, Cyprian was right in urging caution, especially in restoring leaders to their former roles. Callistus, however, was also right in observing that withholding restoration often hinders rather than helps to promote repentance. There is transforming power in the forgiving grace of God, and requiring a lengthy vexing of soul by a repentant sinner seems contrary to Paul's direction to the Corinthians.

ILLUSTRATION

Concerning pastoral leadership, 'Charles Spurgeon recommended that leaders who lapse should step down from the pulpit, sit in the last pew, "and stay there until their repentance is as notorious as their sin".'[6]

Although many would argue that pastors who fail morally should never be readmitted to the pulpit, Spurgeon's advice seems wise, in the light of how God dealt with biblical characters. On 1 May 1988, in a service at Grace Chapel in Lexington, Massachusetts, Gordon MacDonald was restored to ministry after eighteen long months of church discipline for his admitted adultery. His wife, along with church leaders from inside and outside the church, had monitored him throughout this period with a view to seeing him restored. He was not left on his own.

Clearly, timing is important. This is especially true when a sin is discovered. Decisive action is required. Delay makes it more and more difficult to deal with an offence. In the church, no less than in society, justice delayed is justice besmirched. Peter acted decisively in the matter of Ananias and Sapphira's sin. Paul rebuked the Corinthian church for delaying church discipline. But when the discipline achieved its intended end he again rebuked them, this time for delaying the re-instatement of the repentant pair. A difficult balance to attain!

This is no well-oiled, five-step way of dealing quickly with sin. Great patience, agonizing prayer, tearful entreaties and loving discussions may be involved. But when all efforts fail, Christ and his missionary apostle command us to excommunicate unrepentant members. They also command us to restore repentant believers. Failure to maintain this balance has contributed greatly to the current abysmal state of the church.

On a personal level, however, none of us have the corporate authority of the church to exercise discipline. We should be careful not to pre-judge or shun those with whom we have a dispute. If we cut ourselves off from certain believers in a case where the church as a whole has not taken action, we sin presumptuously by acting as if we were the judge. Even in cases of clear sin in others, we must walk a fine line that avoids encouraging the unrepentant in their rebellion but gently points the way of repentance.

Questions for discussion

1. *What are some of the positive purposes served by confronting sinners (church discipline)? (See Galatians 6:1; Ephesians 4:3-6; 1 Corinthians 5:1-2, 6-7.)*

2. *What are some of the specific sins that call for church discipline? (See 1 Corinthians 5:11; 2 Thessalonians 3:6; Titus 3:9-10; 2 John 10-11.)*

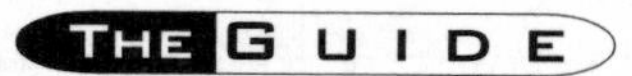

DISCUSS IT

3. *What does Matthew 18:15-17 teach us about the importance of confidentiality?*

4. *Describe the four steps for church discipline given in Matthew 18:15-17.*

5. *Write down verses that teach us about the fifth step, the main goal of church discipline.*

CHAPTER ELEVEN

MUST I FORGIVE THE UNREPENTANT?

LOOK IT UP

BIBLE REFERENCE

'Forgive whatever grievances you may have against one another.
Forgive as the Lord forgave you'
(Colossians 3:13).

INTRODUCTION

Near the end of the film *2000 Acres*, a dying widow makes her sister promise to care for her two children — and pass on the family legacy. The legacy, it turns out, is hostility towards their unrepentant and abusive father. As she dies, she whispers: 'My sole accomplishment in life is that I didn't forgive the unforgivable.'

Refusal to forgive notorious sins is much admired. A recent TV documentary traced the strange story of a husband who abandoned his family, faked his suicide and took up a new life with a false name in a distant place. He left his wife and young children in dire straits. Years later, when he was finally discovered, his wife went to great lengths to bring him to justice. In the courtroom she took satisfaction in demanding a heavy fine and a lengthy prison term. Her teenage children echoed her bitterness. One had to admire the grit with which the abandoned wife built a new life for herself and her children. Leaving aside for the moment the matter of restitution and civil justice, which will be addressed in the next chapter, should she have been willing to forgive him? Some Christians would argue that she should forgive unconditionally. Other Christians would maintain that if he proved unrepentant, she was under no obligation to forgive him.

One example of the contrast in these divergent opinions was reported at the time of an incident relating to Prince Charles. On coming out of the funeral service for his uncle, Lord Mountbatten (who had been blown up by an IRA bomb), at which the Archbishop of Canterbury prayed for forgiveness towards the perpetrators, Prince Charles was reported as saying, 'Why should I forgive them?' Many Christian people feel that he had a point since these people neither asked for nor desired to be forgiven.

Should we forgive people unconditionally or should we withhold forgiveness from those who are unrepentant? To withhold forgiveness seems only fair. We may still feel the sting of Jill's tongue-lashing, or we may live amidst the shattered pieces left by Joe's unfaithfulness, or ... You fill in the blanks. Suppose we seek reconciliation with a person who has grievously slandered us. What do we do if that person not only refuses to accept our offer of forgiveness, but adds to his false accusations? What if the person's expression of sorrow is trite and hollow although the offence was grave?

Let's clarify the two positions Christians hold concerning forgiving the unrepentant.

EXPLANATION

1. No forgiveness without repentance

Those who maintain that we have no duty to forgive the unrepentant make some of the following arguments.

- 'If your brother sins, rebuke him, and if he repents, forgive him. If he sins against you seven times in a day, and seven times comes back to you and says, "I repent," forgive him' (Luke 17:3). This text makes it clear that we should feel no constraint to forgive the unrepentant.
- 'If we confess our sins, he is faithful and just and will forgive us our sins and purify us from all unrighteousness' (1 John 1:9). If our receiving forgiveness from God is contingent on our confession of sin, then so must the forgiveness we give others be contingent on their admitting their sins.
- The passage studied in the previous chapter on church discipline, Matthew 18:15-17, indicates that impenitence on the part of a sinning brother results, not in forgiveness, but in being treated as a 'pagan or a tax collector'.
- 'Forgiving each other, just as in Christ God forgave you' (Ephesians 4:32). The way we forgive others is to be modelled on how God

forgave us. Forgiveness from God is contingent on us demonstrating faith and repentance.
- In the parable of the unforgiving steward, although the forgiveness offered to him was enormous, it was still conditional on his coming to the Master to ask for mercy.
- Jesus' request from the cross, 'Father, forgive them, for they do not know what they are doing' (Luke 23:34), is not an example of his forgiving his crucifiers but of him asking the Father to forgive them. In the following days, many priests, along with the centurion who witnessed the crucifixion, did repent and believe. Their subsequent repentance initiated the Father's forgiveness — an answer to Jesus' prayer. Jesus' statement was not blanket forgiveness but a request that the Father would forgive those who repent.

Gordon Rumford echoes the perspective summarized above. 'If no repentance is evident, [offended people] have no Scriptural command or precedent to forgive the impenitent. All impenitent people will perish forever because God does not forgive until we confess our sins (1 John 1:9). If God says he withholds forgiveness until there is repentance can we institute a different course of action? It seems to me that only those who confessed their sins throughout the Old Testament received forgiveness and it is the same in the New Testament. If God forgives without repentance then we have a form of universalism where everyone is forgiven and in a state of grace. Or, if sometimes God forgives without repentance, he is inconsistent with the teaching of Scripture that calls sinners to repent… Why repent if we can get forgiveness without it?'

Philip Foster also represents this group. In responding to a column I wrote on this subject in *Evangelical Times* he commented: 'When we are faced with someone who has sinned against us, we are called as Christians to pray for them, bless them, love them and never to hold a grudge against them. Yes, we must be instantly ready to forgive them the moment they show sign [sic] of repentance. But we cannot forgive someone who remains unrepentant.'[1]

Christopher Rogers also responded to this column. He seems to come down on both sides of the question. He quotes J. C. Ryle's comment on Luke 17:3: 'if he repents forgive him'. '[This] doubtless cannot mean that we are not to forgive men unless they do repent. At this rate there would be much bitterness constantly alive. But it does mean that where there is no repentance or regret for injury done, there can be no renewal of cordial friendship, or complete reconciliation between man and man.' While he opens the door of forgiveness fairly wide in the first part of the letter, he goes on to ease it towards closure in the rest. 'The words from the cross, "forgive them, for they know not what they do", must have been uttered in the sure knowledge of an eventual repentance on the part of those (and only those) for whom the prayer was offered.'[2]

2. Forgiveness in spite of impenitence

Let me now list some of the arguments and Scriptures used by those who believe we should offer forgiveness indiscriminately, whether the offender repents or not.

- God asked Hosea to buy back his wife from slavery in spite of the fact that she had committed adultery. This was not contingent on her repentance or request for restoration but intended to be an example of the unmerited love of God for Israel. 'The Lord said to me, "Go, show your love to your wife again, though she is loved by another and is an adulteress. Love her as the LORD loves the Israelites, though they turn to other gods and love the sacred raisin cakes." So I bought her' (Hosea 3:1-2).
- Christ taught that our response to others should not be conditioned by how they treat us. '"Love your enemies," he said, "Do good to those who hate you ... pray for those who ill-treat you. If someone strikes you on one cheek, turn to him the other also"' (Matthew 5:44; Luke 6:27-29). Surely, the same principle should be followed in forgiveness. Our treatment of those who sin against us, including our forgiving them, should not be conditioned by their actions towards us; for example, waiting until they repent.

EXPLANATION

- In the explanation Christ gave for the request 'Forgive us our debts, as we also have forgiven our debtors' (Matthew 6:12) he mentions nothing about forgiving only those who confess to us their sins. 'For if you forgive men when they sin against you, your heavenly Father will also forgive you. But if you do not forgive men their sins, your Father will not forgive your sins' (6:14-15). Surely this would be the place to insert an exception to this rule — 'forgive men their sins unless they don't confess them' — if the forgiveness offered depended upon their confession and repentance.
- Although the prodigal in the parable confesses 'Father, I have sinned,' the father did not wait for this expression of repentance before he embraced him. 'While he was still a long way off, his father saw him and was filled with compassion for him; he ran to his son, threw his arms around him and kissed him' (Luke 15:20). Surely one application of this parable ought to be that prodigious expressions of love and compassion can precede the response of an offending person.
- Consider Jesus' words from the cross: 'Father, forgive them, for they do not know what they are doing' (Luke 23:34). At the very least these words express a profound desire by Jesus that those who had collaborated in his crucifixion be forgiven and escape the wrath of God.

Uttered as they are in the midst of unimaginable suffering, do they not call us to demonstrate an attitude of forgiveness even to the worst sinners?

- Jesus' treatment of the woman caught in adultery (John 8:3-11) calls us to offer compassionate forgiveness even to the most notorious sinners. Leon Morris says in his commentary that there is nothing here about forgiveness. True, the word 'forgiveness' is not used, but the message is implicit in the actions of Jesus. While Jesus said, 'Leave your life of sin', indicating that he did not condone sin, he did forgive her: 'Neither do I condemn you' (John 8:11). Freedom from condemnation is just another way of expressing divine forgiveness for sin! And this is offered to the woman in spite of her apparent silence on the subject of repentance. No doubt Christ's compassion moved her to repentance ... but her reception of forgiveness likely preceded her repentant response.
- The query by the disciples, 'Lord, how many times shall I forgive my brother when he sins against me? Up to seven times?' (Matthew 18:21), indicates a desire to limit forgiveness. Jesus' answer, 'I tell you, not seven times, but seventy-seven times' (18:22), teaches that forgiveness is unlimited. But surely a person who asks for forgiveness five or six or even ten times is showing that he is not sincere? At the very least he has a very defective lifestyle! Is an expression such as, 'I repent,' enough, even if the expression is obviously insincere? Christ recognized our inability to read the motives of others.

Since that is the case, it is much wiser to grant forgiveness than to refuse it on the basis of imagined insincerity. To remind accusers of the adulterous woman of this fact, Jesus said, 'If any one of you is without sin, let him be the first to throw a stone at her' (John 8:7).

Is repentance a grace or a work?

'God freely justifies the persons whom He effectually calls. He does this, not by infusing righteousness into them, but by pardoning their sins and by accounting them, and accepting them, as righteous. This He does for Christ's sake alone, and not for anything wrought in them or done by them. The righteousness which is imputed to them, that is, reckoned to their account, is neither their faith nor the act of believing nor any other obedience to the gospel which they have rendered, but Christ's obedience alone... The repentance that leads on to salvation is a gospel grace by means of which a person who is caused by the Holy Spirit to feel the manifold evils of sin is also caused by faith in Christ to humble himself on account of sin.'

Baptist Confession of Faith of 1689– rewritten in Modern English, Haywards Heath: Carey, 1979, pp. 33,38

THINK ABOUT IT

- The mystery of predestination and effectual calling reminds us that we are saved by a gracious act of God taken before we have had a chance to repent. 'In him we have redemption through his blood, the forgiveness of sins, in accordance with the riches of God's grace' (Ephesians 1:7). This forgiveness is entirely dependent on ordination — God's good pleasure, our adoption and union with Christ in his atoning sacrifice (v. 5) and God's choosing (v. 11). See the order in Romans 8:30: predestination, calling, justification, glorification. While repentance and faith are an integral part of conversion, they are not works that move God to save us. They are, themselves, gifts of God given at the new birth (see Ephesians 2:8-10).

I realize that Arminians[3] will disagree with me about this last point. And while this is not the place to enter into a lengthy debate about theology, I find it impossible to read the Scriptures without seeing the sovereign grace of God as the operative power behind our salvation. It is the Holy Spirit whom we must credit, not we ourselves, with moving us to turn from our sins.

On the basis of some, or all, of the biblical content mentioned above, many Christians teach that gospel grace requires us to offer unconditional forgiveness. In his book, *A Forgiving God in an Unforgiving World*, Ron Lee Davis writes: 'What if we have done everything we could to lovingly win our brother and sister over to a restored relationship with ourselves and God? If that person remains unrepentant, should we then withhold forgiveness from him? Absolutely not! We should forgive him continuously and immediately and completely. In fact, we should forgive the person even before we go to confront him or her. A sinner's confession and repentance are prerequisites to healing and reconciliation but not to forgiveness! Forgiveness must be complete and instantaneous and unconditional.'[4] Personally, I think Davis overstates the case. We need a third alternative.

TO SUMMARIZE

Some sincere Christians call us to offer unconditional forgiveness, while others affirm that it is our duty to withhold forgiveness until the guilty party repents.

Those who argue for conditional forgiveness, forgiving only the repentant, point to the passage on church discipline in Matthew 18, explain Jesus' saying from the cross as a prayer fulfilled only in those who repented later and cite Luke 17:3. They explain that 1 John 1:9 makes forgiveness contingent on confession. Since God forgives us when we repent and we are called to forgive as he does, we should not forgive others until they repent.

Those who affirm that the gospel of grace calls us to offer forgiveness without demanding repentance point to God's instructions

TO SUMMARIZE

to Hosea, Jesus' teaching on loving enemies and turning the other cheek, the parable of the prodigal son, Jesus' words from the cross, Jesus' treatment of the woman caught in adultery and the direct and unconditional commands to forgive (e.g. Matthew 6:12,14-15; Ephesians 4:32; Matthew 18:26-27). They also point out that God chose us in love long before we repented of our sins.

3. Lavish forgiveness tempered by specific constraints

The biblical evidence comes down overwhelmingly on the side of lavish forgiveness. It is far better to forgive a person who later shows us his insincerity than to withhold forgiveness from someone who later shows us that he was sincerely struggling to be repentant. I'd rather make a mistake forgiving someone than withholding forgiveness. Surely, our attitude towards sinners should be patterned after the Master's, concerning whom we read: 'A bruised reed he will not break, and a smouldering wick he will not snuff out' (Matthew 12:20). Christ had reason to come down on sinners like a ton of bricks — but he didn't. His gentleness with Peter, with the woman caught in adultery, even with Judas, is astounding. We need to give others the benefit of the doubt by extending forgiveness freely, generously, joyously and fully.

Although we should be willing to err on the side of giving rather than withholding forgiveness, we need to remind ourselves of several principles. These principles will help us avoid either the extreme of conditional forgiveness on the one hand or unconditional forgiveness on the other.

Firstly, we must agree that the injured party, the one sinned against, has a responsibility to gently confront the person who caused the injury with a view to seeking reconciliation. 'If your brother sins rebuke him' (Luke 17:3). Forgiving a person does not mean we do not confront that person.

Secondly, notorious or public sins committed by Christians call for church discipline. (Examples of such sins are listed in the previous chapter.) Churches must withhold forgiveness until there is repentance. 'If he refuses to listen even to the church, treat him as you would a pagan or a tax collector' (Matthew 18:17).

Individuals, however, do not have church authority. Individual offences between people, that do not directly affect the church's testimony, have to be dealt with on a personal basis. Commenting on the 'infinity of forgiving love' in Lange's commentary, Oosterzee writes: 'To the individual brother, there is not permitted what at last may be allowed to the church, namely, to put one out as a publican and heathen.'[5]

Thirdly, distinguishing between God's prerogatives and ours may help to clarify issues. In the moral universe forgiveness is a judicial transaction between the sovereign Judge of all the earth and a repentant sinner. 'Judgement is mine, I will repay, says the Lord.' While we must be discerning, Christ teaches us that judgement, in the sense of condemnation, is not ours to exercise. This counsel is wise since our human limitations make it impossible for us to exercise perfect discernment. Only God knows the true heart condition of those who appear repentant, or unrepentant. He alone knows the heart of man. And thus, in a moral sense, we cannot offer a person the forgiveness that is only God's to give. In the meantime he expects us to forgive 'seventy times seven', which seems to me to be an appeal for us to bend over backwards to forgive. We ought to be generous in our forgiveness, miserly in our unforgiveness.

Fourthly, the word 'forgiveness' is used in different ways. As noted above, in a moral or judicial sense, only God can forgive. Nevertheless we are asked to forgive everything! 'Bear with one another and forgive whatever grievances you may have against one another. Forgive as the Lord forgave you' (Colossians 3:13). What we are called to do here (see v. 8), and in Ephesians 4, is to repudiate 'bitterness, rage and anger, brawling and slander, along with every form of malice. Be kind and compassionate to one another, forgiving' (vv. 31-32).

The forgiveness that God calls us to demonstrate is an attitude, a freedom from resentment, bitterness and malice. A generous spirit repudiates the desire to hurt, to get even, to seek revenge. It lets everyone know that the door of reconciliation is always open. Dr Archibald Hart has suggested that forgiveness is: 'Giving up my right to hurt you for hurting me.' Forgiving people offer

EXPLANATION

to those who have hurt them, a compassionate, accepting attitude that refuses to allow hurts to simmer. Whether or not people accept our forgiveness, or forgive us, we should present to them a 'forgiving face'. From the human viewpoint this constitutes a forgiving spirit.

Fifthly, offering this kind of forgiveness does not mean that we are responsible for resurrecting a ruined relationship. If a person is unrepentant this will be impossible. Indeed, this is the interpretation Matthew Henry puts on Luke 17:3 about forgiveness and repentance. 'Though he do not repent, you must not therefore bear malice to him, nor meditate revenge; but if he do not at least say that he repents, you are not bound to be so free and familiar with him as you have been.'[6] Offering forgiveness may not mean we can restore a relationship that has been damaged.

Sixthly, this kind of 'human forgiveness' does not absolve the forgiven person from taking responsibility for his actions. Nor does it deny the importance of making restitution. Since it involves confrontation and rebuke, it is not cheap grace that treats forgiveness too lightly. Nor does it mean that the 'forgiven person' will not have to suffer the consequences of his or her sin in a civil or church court.

Seventhly, and most importantly, offering abundant forgiveness to an unrepentant person may profoundly influence his subsequent attitude. It was the intervention of God in applying unmerited grace to our hearts that saved us from our sins — and then moved us to respond. Before his grace touched our hearts, we were alienated from God; rebellious; arrogant. But after we were smitten by the gospel of God's love in Christ, we fell to our knees in confession and repentance. We began to respond to the one against whom we had sinned — we began to love and worship him. In human relationships, the demonstration of this kind of undeserved love to impenitent people will touch their hearts.

THINK ABOUT IT

> 'Christians should be of a forgiving spirit, willing to make the best of everybody, and to make all about them easy; forward to extenuate faults, and not to aggravate them; and they should contrive as much to show that they have forgiven an injury as others to show that they resent it.'
>
> Matthew Henry, *Commentary*, p. 765

Mark Thistle of Scarborough, Ontario, was savagely beaten when he mistakenly picked up the wrong change at a tavern. He remained in a coma for five weeks with a brain haemorrhage that left him epileptic, clinically blind, subject to mood swings and memory loss — and out of work. Mark had drifted from his Christian roots. Although he returned to Christ during his recovery, he continually fed the fire of hatred for his attacker. He desperately wanted him to die and go to hell. When he

ILLUSTRATION

heard his attacker's story, however, a desire to forgive welled up within him.

In court he stood and said, 'I've done a lot of thinking about this and in my own heart I bear no animosity. I totally forgive him. This whole experience has been a nightmare, but Jesus Christ has presented himself in my life through it. I've never felt better.'[7] Mark discovered the power of forgiveness! So did his attacker.

Upon hearing his testimony, Mark's attacker began crying in the box. Mark's parents went up to 'comfort him and offer him tissues. "He kept thanking me over and over," Mark says. Because of Mark's testimony, lawyers say the penalty was reduced from a possible ten years to just over three.'[8]

In a recent TV talk show I heard the interviewer comment: 'People who call themselves Christians are the last to forgive.' How can that be? We should be the first to forgive! It is much better to err on the side of mercy, like Mark, than to be harsh, legalistic and unforgiving.

Concerning radical grace, Steve Brown quoted a friend whose advice was: 'Forgive them all and let God decide.'[9]

While we might react against such advice by wisely warning about 'lowering the standards' and 'cheap grace' it has been my observation that we often err more on the side of harshness than compassion. We are legalists at heart.

QUESTIONS FOR DISCUSSION

1. *Summarize in your own words the teaching of the following important verses on forgiveness: Hosea 3:1-2; Matthew 18:15-17, 21-22; Luke 17:3-4; 23:34; Colossians 3:13.*

2. *What is the apparent conflict between these verses that must be reconciled?*

3. *Using biblical texts or examples (or both) explain which of the following statements you personally support. You might want to write out your own statement of belief.*

   a. *Unless repentance is evident the offended party has no scriptural duty to forgive the offender.*
   b. *Whether or not repentance is evident, the offended person has a biblical duty to offer complete and unconditional forgiveness.*
   c. *However we are treated we should present to all (even to those who refuse to admit how they have hurt us), a generous, forgiving spirit that communicates our freedom from bitterness and openness to reconciliation.*

CHAPTER TWELVE

WHAT ABOUT RESTITUTION?

LOOK IT UP

BIBLE REFERENCE

'Zacchaeus stood up and said… "…If I have cheated anybody out of anything, I will pay back four times the amount"' (Luke 19:8).

INTRODUCTION

What actions should we expect from repentant offenders? Can a verbal expression of sorrow for harm done wipe out the past? Is it enough for the one offended to respond to this overture by saying, 'I forgive you'? Some would say, 'Absolutely! Just as salvation is a gift of grace and not of works, so forgiveness is a gift of grace that can never be earned.'

Others call this naiveté. They know first-hand how some people pervert grace by light-heartedly expecting others to absolve them of fault, no matter what they do or how many times they offend. These careless offenders seem to think that the 'magic' words 'I'm sorry,' or 'Forgive me,' free them from the responsibility to repair the damage they have inflicted.

Scripture teaches that the subsequent actions of a repentant person either prove or disprove his sincerity. In summarizing his message to the Gentiles before King Agrippa, Paul explained: 'I preached that they should repent and turn to God and prove their repentance by their deeds' (Acts

26:20). Making restitution proves the genuine nature of a person's repentance.

The reality of Zacchaeus' conversion was attested by what he set out to do after his encounter with Jesus Christ. 'Look, Lord! Here and now I give half of my possessions to the poor, and if I have cheated anybody out of anything, I will pay back four times the amount' (Luke 19:8). Through illumination of the Spirit within him, Zacchaeus realized immediately that salvation did not absolve him from making restitution for his crimes. Upon his confession Jesus responded: 'Today salvation has come to this house ... for the Son of Man came to seek and to save what was lost' (Luke 19:9-10). Real repentance is demonstrated by restitution.

Zacchaeus' example also shows that the offender should not be browbeaten into action. He should initiate restitution. The awakened conscience of the repentant person, inextricably connected as it is to his faith in God, moves him to action. Followers of Christ identify with the apostle Paul who said, 'I strive always to keep my conscience clear before God and man' (Acts 24:16).

THINK ABOUT IT

'Restitution is always unilateral — always one-sided. Never look for the other person to take the blame or even share in the blame. Restitution is specifically a matter of settling my wrongness... By understanding my sole responsibility to make restitution, I may move straight to the issue,

EXPLANATION

> avoiding the snare of thinking that I must first establish a certain kind of delicate "treaty" with the other party.'
>
> Ralph Sutera, *Restitution Guidelines,* Regina: Canadian Revival Fellowship, undated.

The Scriptures are clear. 'If anyone sins and is unfaithful to the LORD by deceiving his neighbour about something entrusted to him or left in his care or stolen, or if he cheats him, or if he finds lost property and lies about it... He must return what he has stolen or taken by extortion, or what was entrusted to him, or the lost property he found... He must make restitution in full, add a fifth of the value to it and give it all to the owner' (Leviticus 6:1-5). 'When a man or woman wrongs another in any way and so is unfaithful to the LORD, that person is guilty and must confess the sin he has committed. He must make full restitution for his wrong, add one fifth to it and give it all to the person he has wronged' (Numbers 5:6-7). In Exodus a thief is asked to 'pay back double' (22:4).

We must do everything in our power to right any wrongs we have committed. And this is not a time, as Zacchaeus realized, to be legalistic about the extent of our restitution — whether we add a fifth, double the amount, or restore it fourfold — we need to be generous.

Consider several scenarios. A Christian woman tells her friends stories that prove untrue about another woman. A girl helps herself to grapes from a vineyard on her way home from school. A boy steals money from his father's drawer. A man works Saturdays as a handyman, but fails to declare the income to the tax office. A boy pilfers items from a store. A man brags about a supervisory position he does not have.

I was the boy who pilfered. When I was converted God compelled me to go to the store, confess my stealing and offer to pay it back. (The manager was so astounded he refused any repayment.)

The slanderous woman must go to those to whom she told lies in order to correct the facts she distorted. She must also confess her fault to the one she slandered. The boy must go to his father, admit his stealing and repay what he took. The handyman must report all his income to the tax office and pay any tax or penalty due. The man who bragged about an imaginary supervisory position must go to those to whom he told his lie in order to correct the facts.

What about the girl who stole the grapes? When Beulah Petersen was nine years old she began to help herself to bunches of juicy Tokay grapes on her way home from school. Twenty years later she was a Sunday school teacher. One Sunday, as she drove past the vineyard on her way to teach her class, her conscience prompted her: 'How do you expect to tell young people to follow and obey the Lord if you fail to do so yourself?'

After a great internal struggle, she stopped the car, turned around and pulled into the vineyard. With trepidation, she knocked on the door of the farmhouse.

ILLUSTRATION

When she was invited in, she blurted out to the man seated there: 'I ... I used to steal grapes from you when I was child ... I'm a Christian now and I want to make it right.' He looked at her strangely, then sent her to talk to his wife.

Beulah repeated her confession to the wife and then handed her some money as restitution. Later she discovered that the man was an atheist. Before long the Holy Spirit again constrained her to visit the farmhouse. This time the wife welcomed her eagerly and invited her to share about Jesus Christ. That very day the wife bowed in submission to the Saviour. Several days later she invited Beulah back to tell the same message to several of her friends.[1]

Some sins cause concrete damage that can be repaired. Nehemiah demanded that the nobles and officials return all the property and even the interest they had exacted from their own people during a time of famine (Nehemiah 5:1-12). Pilfered grapes can be paid for. A stolen stereo can be replaced; unpaid taxes remitted; damage to property repaired. Even the effects of slander can, to some extent, be corrected.

Some damage, however, is much more difficult to put right. Suppose that the actions of a mining company result in many of their workers contracting cancer. A drunken driver kills a family. Children of a chain-smoking father develop breathing problems. A bank robber murders a teller. A wife has an affair. A father abuses his children. A woman sells her body as a prostitute. What actions should be expected of repentant offenders in cases such as these?

Restitution for some sins is impossible. People murdered or killed in an accident cannot be brought back to life. A company responsible for cancer in their workers cannot restore them to full health. The damage caused by abuse, rape, or adultery cannot be erased by repentant words from the perpetrator. A converted prostitute can hardly express remorse to any of her 'clients'.

Each situation calls for a different kind of restitution. The drunken driver could do something to provide for the family he shattered or contribute to a programme to eradicate the problem caused by those who drink and drive. The justice system administers punishment that varies with the perceived intent and guilt of the offender. A mining company might be severely fined or have the fine moderated if they have acknowledged their blame, begun to pay compensation to workers and endow scholarships for their families. Tobacco companies have recently been held liable for lung cancer.

We cannot make restitution for sins that we commit in the privacy of our own hearts. Pride and prejudice: a woman despises a poorly dressed immigrant; covetousness: a Christian man covets his neighbour's boat; resentment: a daughter-in-law resents the unwanted advice of her mother-in-law; hatred: a boy hates a teacher who humiliated him in class; lust: a man imagines an affair with his secretary.

Private sins should remain private. If our sinful thoughts have not spawned overt words or actions they should be confessed to God alone. We must never go up to a person and say something like: 'Forgive me, I have really been resentful of your advice'; or, 'I've had lustful thoughts about you'; or, 'I've despised you.' Such a confession is likely to create untold harm.

The evangelist Ralph Sutera writes: 'Deal with God alone about private sins of the mind and body. These should never be included in restitution. When the other party knows nothing about it, deal only with God… Go to the other party only when he clearly knows about the situation. If you have shared these thoughts or feelings with a third party, go to him and let him know you have made this right with God. Go no further under any circumstances. Some have "created" thoughts in the other party's mind that were not there previously and "created" a further problem, resulting in bitterness and resentment. Private lustful thoughts expressed to the other party can generate these same thoughts in his mind and precipitate a sinful immoral relationship. Be very careful.'[2]

There are an infinite number of scenarios. Each will require the penitent offender to pray for wisdom about how to right the wrongs he caused. Every case, however, will require the guilty party to express grief and remorse to those he has harmed. This will usually entail a personal meeting with those he has hurt. It may help if a pastor mediates such a meeting. Sutera comments: 'The general rule is to deal person-to-person. If impossible, telephone. Letters should be a last resort.'[3]

In 1971 Bob Harvey started a teen programme in a neighbourhood church in Edmonton, Canada. Soon after it was up and thriving, one teen confessed that 'he and several other bored 13- and 14-year-olds had broken into several nearby homes. My co-leader and I met with these young offenders and suggested we go in a group to the homes they had broken into and apologize. The homeowners had suffered damage to their homes, loss of property, and a sense of violation, and the teens quickly realized it wasn't enough just to say they were sorry. Soon we were conducting bottle drives and car washes so the teens could at least pay back the cash they had stolen... That was the last crime committed by any of those teens, and their victims became some of their biggest supporters.'[4]

The Edmonton police warned the teens about what might have happened if they had not worked so hard to repair the damage. Fortunately, in this case they did not press charges.

Christian forgiveness is not meant to circumvent a country's justice system. Paul points out that civil authorities receive their mandate from God. 'He is God's servant, an agent of wrath to bring punishment on the wrongdoer' (Romans 13:4). Where the offence involves civil or criminal prosecution the offender must be ready to accept punishment. Mark Thistle's attacker, as mentioned in chapter 11, was sentenced in a court of law.

ILLUSTRATION

Personally, I believe that God has mandated the death penalty for heinous capital crimes as a necessary social deterrent for acts of violence. Punitive justice is clearly biblical but so is 'restorative justice'.[5] Unfortunately, many evangelical Christians see justice only in terms of retribution and not rehabilitation. But our God is both just and merciful.

Since the Christian gospel is redemptive, surely our concern for criminals should not end with their punishment. The love of Christ has led many Christians to intervene in criminal cases with a view to transforming the criminal. On an April evening in 1958, a twenty-six-year-old Korean exchange student named In Ho Oh was brutally assaulted on his way to post a letter. He later died at a nearby hospital. The Philadelphia police soon arrested the gang of teenagers involved.

News of this senseless killing angered people across North America. From Korea, Ho's parents wrote the authorities in Philadelphia an astonishing letter. 'We thank God that He has given us a plan whereby our sorrow is being turned into Christian purpose. It is our hope that we may somehow be instrumental in the salvation of the souls … of the murderers. Our family has met together and we have decided to petition that the most generous treatment possible within the laws of your government be given to those who have committed this criminal action… Our whole family has decided to save money to start a fund to be used for the religious, educational, and social guidance of the boys when they are released.'[6]

These Korean Christians were extending revolutionary love towards their son's murderers. Their action is reflective of what some Christians are calling 'restorative justice'. Bob Harvey and his co-worker took this route in dealing with the teenage thieves in Edmonton. As described previously, Mark Thistle's forgiveness melted his attacker's heart and resulted in a reduced sentence. Sydna Massé's approach to Jennie, her friend's murderer, contributed to her amazing transformation. Jennie was converted and Sydna was led to commence a ministry to women in prison (see chapter 5).

You may be thinking at this point: 'Wait a minute. What about the victims?' You would be quite right in pointing out that attempts to rehabilitate criminals must take into account the pain felt by their victims. Pierre Allard, a Baptist minister, head of the chaplaincy service of Canada's federal Correctional Services, is a passionate advocate of 'making inmates accountable to their victims and then reintegrating them into the community'. He points out that criminals must realize that their crimes inject brokenness into a community. Since 'real people have hurt real people' there must be a listening to all parties. This includes not only the offender, but also the victim and the families that have been hurt. Allard says, 'There can be no restorative justice if there is not an expression of hurt by the victim and an acknowledgement by the perpetrator of what he has done.'[7]

THINK ABOUT IT

This ought not to be a concept alien to Christians. Forgiveness calls for listening, confrontation, repentance, sorrow for sin and making restitution. According to Allard, restorative justice used to be part of the Judeo-Christian tradition as exemplified by Augustine. In the fifth century Augustine wrote to a judge about to sentence the murderers of a Christian friend. 'He implored the judge not to avenge the death "by the infliction of precisely similar injuries in the way of retaliation... Rather be moved by the wounds these thieves have inflicted on their own souls to exercise a desire to heal them."'[8]

THINK ABOUT IT

An Angus Reid poll suggests that willingness to offer forgiveness to others depends on the degree of hurt experienced. Among monthly churchgoers, 71% believe that 'God is very understanding and forgiving' but only 3% would eventually be willing to forgive a drunk driver who killed one of their family members. The statistics improve somewhat among weekly church attendees of whom 93% believe that God is understanding and very forgiving. Only 26% of these, however, feel they would eventually be able to forgive a drunken homicide.

Don Posterski, 'Forgive, or else', *Christian Week*, 1 April 1997, p. 7

The Christian approach to restitution does not demand the 'eye for an eye and a tooth for a tooth' kind of justice codified in the Mosaic Law (Exodus 21:24). Even in the Old Testament, murderers such as Moses and David, although severely disciplined by God, received forgiveness instead of the death penalty.

Clearly, victims of negligence and crime cannot adequately deal with their hurt and loss without massive infusions of divine grace. It is easier to write about this subject than imagine the grief suffered by someone who has lost a loved one due to another's carelessness or malice. I do not mean to trivialize the anguish victims feel. Most of us have no idea how we would act in similar circumstances. I certainly don't. But I trust that the Holy Spirit would help me supernaturally to respond with a forgiveness like that of the Jastremskis.

In June 1999 Stephen Stacey struck and killed Sabine Jastremski. The accident occurred when he failed to stop at a rural junction near Pembroke, Ontario. Stacey automatically lost his licence for a year. James Scott, co-ordinator of a new pilot project, the collaborative justice project, arranged for Stephen to meet the grief-stricken parents. Stephen expressed sincere sorrow. The parents responded with forgiveness. Walter Jastremski explained: 'We can't get our daughter back. Our good life was destroyed. We have to find a new life without our daughter. If this fellow turns his life around, then we have all gained.' Judge Belanger sentenced Stacey to 200 hours of volunteer work and required him to send two underprivileged children to summer camp — maintaining the charitable tradition of his victim, Sabine Jastremski. In explaining the verdict, Belanger said, 'I commend the Jastremski family for their forgiving nature and their outstanding generosity and courage.'[9]

The Jastremskis' forgiveness paved the way for Stacey's rehabilitation. Without approaching sin and crime redemptively, what hope can we offer to the nightmare of alienation that shatters many of our communities? How can we expect Roman Catholics and Protestants in Northern Ireland, for example, to hammer out some kind of peace if we do not demonstrate forgiveness on a personal level?

Is there any hope of these principles working on an international scale, especially where grotesque horrors have been perpetrated on one race by another? Think of centuries of ethnic violence in Yugoslavia, Stalin's purges, the red terror in China. As mentioned earlier, Philip Yancey cites examples of races at enmity with each other who have learned to forgive. Polish Christians, at first adamant about refusing to forgive Germans, have established friendships with West German Christians. In Russia, Yancey heard with his own ears General Stolyarov of the KGB admitting that 'Political questions cannot be decided until there is sincere repentance, a return to faith by the people.'[10]

The first action of the free East German parliament was to pass a statement asking 'all the

Jews of the world to forgive us'. Before this, West Germany had repented officially for Nazi abominations and paid out sixty billion dollars in reparation to Jews. Yancey writes: 'The fact that a relationship exists at all between Germany and Israel is a stunning demonstration of transnational forgiveness. Grace has its own power, even in international politics.'[11]

THINK ABOUT IT

> 'Forgiveness is neither easy nor clear-cut... The pope may forgive his assassin but not ask for his release from prison. One may forgive the Germans but put restrictions on armies, forgive a child abuser but keep him away from his victims, forgive Southern racism but enforce laws to keep it from happening again.'
>
> Philip Yancey, *What's So Amazing About Grace?*

Those who sincerely repent will express their remorse and regret to the person, or nation, they have harmed. If their action was a civil or criminal crime they will have to accept the punishment that is meted out. They will do everything possible to repair the damage they have caused. They will walk the pathway towards reformation and restoration. They may even discover reconciliation with those they have harmed.

DISCUSS IT

QUESTIONS FOR DISCUSSION

1. *Summarize the Old Testament laws about restitution as indicated in the following verses: Exodus 22:4; Leviticus 6:1-5; Numbers 5:6-7.*

2. *Repentance is a change of heart towards sin. But none of us can read the hearts of others — they are invisible. According to Paul in Acts 26:20 how is genuine repentance demonstrated?*

3. *How did Zacchaeus demonstrate his repentance? What is there about his story that shows how the New Testament approach to this subject differs from the Old Testament? (Luke 19:1-8).*

4. *Give three or four examples of each of the following three categories of sins/crimes: those that call for restitution, those for which no restitution is possible, and those that call for civil or criminal punishment.*

5. *What sins should remain private?*

6. *Prove that the biblical concept of justice involves not only retribution or punishment but also rehabilitation and mercy.*

THE GUIDE

CHAPTER THIRTEEN

HOW CAN I DEAL WITH MY WOUNDED EMOTIONS?

LOOK IT UP

BIBLE REFERENCE

'Therefore, since we have been justified through faith, we have peace with God through our Lord Jesus Christ, through whom we have gained access by faith into this grace in which we now stand. And we rejoice in the hope of the glory of God' (Romans 5:1-2).

INTRODUCTION

Our feelings often override our rational self. Even though we know better, we blurt something out that hurts another, and pay the price for weeks — or years. Envious, we slip in a slur against someone that we know to be unkind as soon as it has left our lips. Feelings get us into all kinds of hot water.

Our emotions can also act as a drag keeping us from soaring aloft in the clean, pure air of forgiveness. When we are the one receiving forgiveness, we know that we should feel forgiven but guilt drags us back into a swamp of recrimination. When we are the offended party, we know that we should forget how others have hurt us, but the memories return and we sink back into a bog of resentment.

In this chapter I want to address these problems from two perspectives — from that of the one forgiven; and of the one who forgives. First, what can be done to alleviate guilty feelings that continue to unsettle the forgiven party? 'How can I forgive myself?' Second, what can the forgiver do to stop memories of the hurt continuing to disrupt his consciousness? 'How can I forget?'

1. How can I forgive myself?

Guilt is healthy if it exposes actions contrary to the will of God. Unfortunately, whenever we revert to our natural, pre-regenerate state of mind most of the guilt we feel is defective. Natural religion, in contrast to revealed religion, is based on earning merit. Guilt that is not biblically informed moves us to try to atone for our sins. Whether we choose Shamanism, Spiritism, Hinduism, Buddhism, Islam, Sikhism, or non-biblical forms of Christianity we will face a similar mantra. 'Appease this spirit or that.' 'Wash in this river.' 'Dress this way or that.' 'Say 100 Hail Marys.' 'Follow the six-fold path.' 'Keep the fast.' 'Obey the five pillars of practice.' 'Adopt these moral principles.' 'Do penance.'

If we live under the influence of any of these human religions, our sense of being forgiven will depend upon what we do to atone for our offences. We will likely embrace some kind of penance to dispel guilt. Those who do not have some kind of religious ritual of penance may choose to flagellate themselves emotionally.

The Christian faith is completely different. It is grace from beginning to end. Freedom from guilt is based on receiving a gift, completely undeserved. The penitent is simply to trust in Jesus' sacrifice to have his guilt taken away. Jesus' works, his righteousness, is credited to the sinner's account. 'To the man who does not work but trusts God who justifies the wicked, his faith is credited as righteousness ... David says the same thing... "Blessed are they whose transgressions are forgiven, whose sins are covered"' (Romans 4:5-7). In case you are thinking that such a doctrine just promotes more sin, let me hasten to quote the apostle: 'By no means! We died to sin; how can we live in it any longer?' (Romans 6:2). Every sinner who receives revolutionary grace is transformed by that grace into one who hates sin and happily 'does good works'.

THINK ABOUT IT

Christian forgiveness enshrines the same revolutionary grace that saves us. It is an undeserved gift freely given, humbly received.

Since receiving something so valuable seems too easy, we all have recurrent troubles feeling forgiven or being forgiving. If we wish to learn to accept forgiveness from other human beings, we must first learn to accept God's forgiveness.

A couple wrote to the Radio Bible Class counselling department: 'My husband and I are born again, but we both sinned before our marriage. I even had an abortion. We want our lives to count for the Lord, but we can't forget how terribly we sinned against Him. I'm not sure God has forgiven us.'[1]

Many a sensitive soul knows how they felt. Accepting God's offer of unconditional forgiveness without years of remorse seems to reflect a callous disregard for the sinfulness of sin; it is as if we are too flippant about God's righteous law. Somehow it seems more pious to flagellate our consciences, bemoan our past, and face the world with faces darkened by despair. After all, how can someone who catches a glimpse of the horrors resident in his own selfish heart be joyful?

Grace does not ignore the importance of this kind of self-knowledge, as we saw in chapter two. I am assuming that if you have read this far, you are a humble believer who makes a practice of confessing your sins to God. I assume that you show real repentance. I also assume that you are doing everything in your power to make restitution to those you have harmed. Those who are obstinately rebellious and unrepentant cannot know peace of heart.

Nevertheless we dishonour God if we question his right to give us salvation freely. We reproach God if we try to earn what is free. People have always found free grace too good to be true. Augustine struggled with his immoral past. Martin Luther's lacerated conscience drove him to seek solace through crawling on his knees up the twenty-eight steps of the Scala Sancta in Rome. Despair over his career as captain of a slave ship tormented John Newton.

Fortunately, God won each of their hearts and forgave their sins for Jesus' sake. Newton wrote his ode to amazing grace. Luther's discovery of justification by faith alone sparked the Protestant Reformation.

We will never be able to forgive ourselves properly without understanding how justification transforms lives. We have celebrated this wonder in chapter three. It bears repeating. In his lectures on Galatians Luther wrote: 'If we lose the doctrine of justification, we lose simply everything... Grace and peace — these two words embrace the whole of Christianity. Grace forgives sin, and peace stills the conscience.'[2]

In a born-again child of God, failure to forgive oneself is the fruit of an untaught conscience. It is a failure to trust in the finished work of Christ. Admittedly, the fact that the thrice holy God could cast our sins into the deepest sea, clothe us in the righteousness of Christ, adopt us into his family and call us saints is incredible! But it is true. Dr John Moore comments concerning that sea of forgetfulness where God has cast our sins: 'God has erected a sign. It reads, "No fishing."'

In his commentary on Galatians, Luther describes how we try vainly to justify ourselves by doing something — instead of accepting that we can do nothing. The cleansing of our record in God's sight he calls 'passive righteousness ... for here we work nothing, render nothing to God; we only receive and permit someone else to work in us, namely God. Therefore it is appropriate to call the righteousness of faith, or Christian righteousness, "passive". This is a righteousness hidden in a mystery, which the world does not understand. In fact, Christians themselves do not adequately understand it or grasp it in the midst of their temptations. Therefore it must always be taught and continually exercised. And anyone who does not grasp or take hold of it in afflictions and terrors of conscience cannot stand. For there is no comfort of conscience so solid and certain as this passive righteousness.'[3]

Our sense of being forgiven is proportional to our appreciation of the justifying grace of God who credited 'passive righteousness' to our account the moment we were saved. Conversely, our misery is proportionate to how much we look to our own works to justify us. When we tread this latter pathway, the devil leads us to flog ourselves for our sins and failures — past and present. This accuser hates the truth of justification. If he cannot drown us in blatant licentiousness, he labours to entangle us in a web we construct from our own efforts to please God. The only escape is to flee to Christ with an appeal to his atoning blood — a move that leads Satan to flee in alarm.

Whether we can forgive ourselves, or not, boils down to several simple questions. Do we believe the devil, that liar? Do we believe our feelings, so irrational? Or do we believe God, and embrace unmerited forgiveness with the joy that is our heritage?

Paul urges us to protect our hearts with the breastplate of righteousness; that is, we are to soothe our emotions by faith in God's provision of what Luther calls 'passive righteousness'. Instead of focusing on whether we feel forgiven or not, we need to look to what God has said. And he says of all who are in Christ

Jesus, 'You are forgiven for Jesus' sake.' Whatever our sins might have been: gossip, stealing, drunkenness, hypocrisy, abortion, adultery, violence, even murder, they are washed away by the blood of Christ the instant we are saved. Therefore, 'whenever our hearts condemn us', we need to remember that 'God is greater than our hearts, and he knows everything' (1 John 3:20). 'There is therefore no condemnation for those who are in Christ Jesus' (Romans 5:1; 8:1). Then let's rejoice in our forgiveness, the unmerited gift of free grace!

What is true about God's forgiveness should be true about the forgiveness Christians offer to others. If another person forgives us, we should humbly receive their forgiveness as a gift of grace. Before confessing our sin to the one we have hurt, we will have confessed to God. Concerning this latter confession we know that 'If we confess our sins, he is faithful and just and will forgive us our sins and purify us from all unrighteousness' (1 John 1:9). Think of it! Confession results in instantaneous forgiveness. Since our sins are first and foremost against God, having them dealt with relieves us of a tremendous burden of guilt.

In our human relationships, however, those we have sinned against will not be as perfect in their forgiveness as God. We should not expect it of them. Who are we to demand perfection of another? The residue of our sins will linger in their memories and in their lives. They will struggle to forgive and to forget, as we will see later in this chapter.

We must be patient with others. While we gently work to restore our relationships with those we have hurt, we can draw solace from our Lord Jesus Christ. Our thoughts should often be upon the cross where Jesus bore our sins. We should rejoice in 'the blood of Jesus, his Son, [that] purifies us from all sin' (1 John 1:7). The more we become 'Christ-centred' and 'cross-centred' the more our hearts will be free from guilt and gloom. With Paul we can resolve 'to know nothing while I was with you except Jesus Christ and him crucified' (1 Corinthians 2:2). Our experience of the healing touch of Jesus to our soul will prepare us to treat others as he has treated us.

Consider the prodigal son. After squandering his inheritance on wild living, the prodigal was forced to grovel for food among the pigs he fed. In this state of misery and hunger 'he came to his senses'. On his way back to his father, he went over in his mind the confession he would make: 'I have sinned against heaven and against you. I am no longer worthy to be called your son; make me like one of your hired men' (Luke 15:18-19).

Something in our psyches makes us believe that God cannot erase our past and give us a completely new beginning. Like the prodigal son we stubbornly think we can earn God's approval by becoming his 'hired man'. So we attend church more often; pray longer; read more of the Bible; volunteer in a food bank; double our charitable giving. The soul is very subtle. By doing

EXPLANATION

something, we salvage something of our tattered pride.

We do the same with others that we have hurt. We try to earn their forgiveness. Parents buy their children toys to atone for their absences. Men bring expensive presents to the wives they have betrayed. But the Bible is clear. Nothing we do can atone for sin. A good work today does not erase an evil committed yesterday.

The father in the parable illustrates how God receives us. Even before the prodigal son had a chance to make his confession: 'While he was still a long way off, his father saw him and was filled with compassion for him; he ran to his son, threw his arms around him and kissed him' (Luke 15:20). Although the son made his confession, the father scarcely heard. 'But the father said to his servants, "Quick! Bring the best robe and put it on him. Put a ring on his finger and sandals on his feet. Bring the fattened calf and kill it. Let's have a feast and celebrate"' (Luke 15:22-23).

TO SUMMARIZE

Guilty feelings will keep us from soaring aloft in the pure air of forgiveness. Guilt is healthy when it leads us to confess sin to God. It is unhealthy when it clings to us after God has forgiven us. And he forgives instantly all those who confess their sins to him in reliance on Christ.

All the world's religions are based on doing something to atone for our misdeeds. The Christian knows there is nothing he can do to atone for his sins. Instead, the Christian relies on who God is and what he has done through the sacrifice of Christ on the cross. He simply receives forgiveness as a gift of grace — totally undeserved.

When immature, the Christian often feels that this is too easy. He or she tries to do something to earn the right to feel forgiven. This is the flesh trying to salvage some pride. But we dishonour God if we try to earn what is free.

The more a Christian understands justification — the crediting to his account of the righteousness of Christ — the more he or she can enjoy the feelings of forgiveness that are our heritage. Christians who struggle with their feelings of guilt should meditate often on biblical passages describing God's love, the parable of the prodigal son, the sacrifice of Christ, our justification. They should earnestly ask the Holy Spirit to align their hearts with the biblical facts.

How do we get rid of the guilt that dogs our footsteps even after our confession? Think about how the father in the parable acted. That is how God acts towards us at the first indication of a desire to return to him in repentance. He throws his arms around us with joyful acceptance. There is celebration. His love knows no bounds. We must not trust our feelings; we must trust our Father. 'God is greater than our hearts, and he knows everything' (1 John 3:20).

The treatment meted out by the father is also a lesson about how we should receive those who come to us to apologize for their actions. We should forgive them freely, abundantly, unhesitatingly and with joyful fervour! Sound impossible? It was for just such human impossibilities that Jesus sent the Holy Spirit to dwell within us. That same Spirit will also help us to forget the offences done to us.

2. How can I forget what others have done?

While preaching on forgiving and forgetting, C. H. Spurgeon commented: 'No one burying a mad dog leaves the tail sticking out!' When we forgive, we bury the beast of bitterness. Unfortunately, too often we mark the grave so we can return to brood.

Jenny explained: 'I can forgive her, but I can't forget.' She knew that to accept her friend's apology for biting words uttered in anger was only right, but deep inside she felt that to forget the incident would somehow diminish her strength of character. It would show that she was weak and wishy-washy. In her mind, forgiveness and forgetfulness are not the Siamese twins proclaimed by the gospel.

Who am I to point out this glaring inconsistency in another? Mary Helen and I love each other very much, with a love that grows deeper as the years go by. With forty years of marriage behind us, however, we still have our spats. Sometimes the iron of our independent personalities — which is meant to sharpen our companionship — generates sparks that ignite a smouldering fire. At these times we find ourselves unconsciously reaching back into our memories for some incident that we can use as a weapon. You know the kind of thing I'm talking about. 'You never do...'; 'Yes, but you always...' You fill in the blanks.

How can this be? The file marked 'Forgiven incidents' should be empty! Whenever we forgive, the record of that incident should go through the shredder. Unfortunately our memories create a series of back-up copies filed all over the place and written with indelible ink. And when the sparks fly, they glow with malevolent light.

Clearly, we need radical help. Fortunately, we have it in the person of the Holy Spirit who lives within all God's forgiven people. At the core of the work that he performs is the application of the blood of Christ to our personal hurts. As we submit to him, he slowly, very slowly, transforms us into the image of Christ. That image includes a radical forgetfulness of past wrongs. The divine forgetfulness that we are to emulate is one of the most amazing attributes of our Redeemer. How enlivening to meditate on the fact that God has cast our sins into the deepest sea and remembers them no more. He has removed them from us as far as the east is from the west. What a God we serve!

ILLUSTRATION

Emulating his forgetfulness is not easy. It will usually require us to make deliberate choices. Before he was enthroned, Louis XII of France was cast into prison and kept in chains. Upon his ascension to power, advisers urged him to seek revenge. In answer to their entreaties, he prepared a scroll on which he listed all who had perpetrated crimes against him. Opposite every man's name he inscribed a cross in red ink. Fearing for their lives, his enemies fled. Then the king explained: 'The cross which I drew beside each name was not a sign of punishment but a pledge of forgiveness extended for the sake of the crucified Saviour, who upon His cross forgave His enemies and prayed for them.'[4]

Are we holding grudges against any? We need to deliberately mark a cross by each name, pray for them and ask the Father to help us forget the offence, for Jesus' sake.

In a biblical sense, learning to forget past wrongs is not developing an indifference towards them. Before there can be forgiveness — and its fruit, forgetfulness — there has to be a facing up to the offence. Seeking to forget is not some kind of evangelical amnesia that will enable us to avoid gently confronting the person who has sinned against us. As we've already established, if someone has harmed us and makes no move to put the matter right, we must go to them seeking reconciliation. Putting the offence out of our minds comes after, not before, face-to-face discussion of the offence.

Forgetful forgiveness comes after we meet with the one who has sinned against us. It occurs when we stop reviewing the events surrounding a grievance. We bury them, seal them beneath a tombstone and walk away. Unfortunately, most of us like to keep revisiting the graveyard.

THINK ABOUT IT

> 'Before we can forgive and forget, both offender and offended must remember together, recall the wrongdoing together, finish the feelings together, reconstruct the relationship together and then they may forget together. In the remembering, reconstructing, forgiving and forgetting each regains the other.'
>
> Frank Stagg, *Polarities of man's Existence in Biblical Perspective*, Philadelphia: Westminster, 1973, p. 161
>
> [Cited in Augsburger, p. 45]

Corrie Ten Boom struggled to forget a wrong. She had forgiven the person, but kept rehashing the incident at night upon her bed. After two sleepless weeks she cried out to God for help. Help came in the form of a kindly Lutheran pastor. When she related her problem to him, he pointed to the bell tower. He explained that after the sexton let go of the bell rope, the bell would keep on swinging — DING, DONG, DINg, Dong, d-i-n-g. The notes would get slower and slower and quieter and quieter until finally with a last ding the sound stopped.

He said, 'I believe it is the same with forgiveness — when we forgive we let go the rope, but if we've been tugging at our grievances for a long time, we mustn't be surprised if the old angry thoughts keep coming for a while. They're just the ding dongs of the old bell slowing down.'[5]

And so it proved to be with Corrie. She felt a few more midnight reverberations, a couple of dings when the subject came up in conversations. But the force of the anger dissipated as Corrie's willingness to hang on to the matter disappeared. They finally stopped.

We must choose to let go of the bell-rope of anger and bitterness. By an act of the will, and a cry to God for help, we must turn immediately from bitter thoughts the moment they arise in our minds. Sweet forgetfulness will gradually overpower the memories and suffuse our lives with tenderness towards others.

What of unresolved offences? Suppose all our attempts at reconciliation have been rebuffed. Suppose time has gone by without any confession of wrongdoing by the one who has hurt us? Does stubborn rejection by the offending party give us leave to cherish our memories, to rehash the details, to frame them and hang them up in a prominent place in our memory gallery?

After the American Civil War, Robert E. Lee visited a Kentucky lady. She bitterly pointed out to him the devastation caused by Federal artillery fire to the grand old tree in her front yard. She turned to Lee expecting some word of sympathy and some condemnation for the North. Instead Lee said, 'Cut it down, my dear madam, and forget it.'[6] Lee's lesson is clear. It is better to cast past injustices into the sea of forgetfulness than let their bitter memories keep on poisoning our lives.

How can we forget the pain others have caused us? How can we stem the tide of guilt we feel for the pain we have inflicted on others? Whether we are the forgiver or the forgiven, the very best antidote we can find for troubled hearts is the same. It is to look to the cross. It is to celebrate the forgiveness of God. God is so much greater than our hearts, and his worship so much more important than our grievances, let us be taken up with his love. Let us smother our hurt feelings beneath a paean of praise.

QUESTIONS FOR DISCUSSION

1. *After reading 1 John 1:5 – 2:2 answer the following questions:*

   a. *From the description in these verses, who should feel guilty about sin but often does not?*
   b. *Who should not feel guilty about sin?*
   c. *What is the basis, objective to ourselves, of our right/ duty, to feel forgiven?*

DISCUSS IT

2. *The conscience plays a key role in either making us feel guilty or joyful or indifferent to what we do. What do the following verses tell us about the conscience?*

   a. *Romans 2:14-15*
   b. *1 Corinthians 8:4, 7*
   c. *Titus 1:15*
   d. *1 Timothy 4:1-2*

3. *According to Romans 5:1-2 what is the basis of genuine peace and joy?*

4. *As Christians we are urged to live with a 'clear' or a 'good conscience'. Since we are not robots, however, our feelings often blind us to the facts of our redemption as declared by God. According to Hebrews 10:19-25 what are some of the things we can do to help ourselves, and others, know freedom from a guilty conscience?*

5. *What are some of the reasons why we may find it difficult to forget how others have hurt us?*

6. *What are some of the redemptive facts mentioned in Hebrews 10:19-25 of which we need to remind ourselves if we have trouble forgetting what others have done to us?*

THE GUIDE

CHAPTER FOURTEEN

SHOULD I ASK FORGIVENESS FOR MY ANCESTORS?

LOOK IT UP

BIBLE REFERENCE

'The son will not share the guilt of the father, nor will the father share the guilt of the son' (Ezekiel 18:20).

INTRODUCTION

Mary Helen, my lifelong helpmate, grew up as a white female in the segregated society of the U.S. South. With the help of black sharecroppers,[1] her parents worked a small farm in South Carolina. Does God expect her to confess sins that promoted slavery and white oppression?

Many Christians would answer 'Yes'. Rudy and Marny Pohl write: 'Unconfessed sins in the distant past, and the unresolved guilt and unhealed wounds which have resulted, have carried forward through generations to poison our present and jeopardize our future.'[2] They assert that we must humbly confess the wrongs committed by our group against other groups for the love of Jesus to break down the strongholds of generational sin. Vancouver pastor David M. Damien of Watchman for the Nations believes that Canada must repent of anti-Semitism before French-English conflicts or those with the First Nations can be resolved. Confession of generational sin, in his view, will precede revival. He says, 'It is time for nations to put the plumb line out to where they stand with the Jews.' He particularly highlights the way Jews were treated by Canada during World War Two. Canada joined Cuba and the U.S.A. in turning away the *St Louis,* loaded with 900 Jewish refugees, and sending them back to Germany. The elder of a Baptist church was the director of Canada's immigration branch that made that fateful decision. Three members of parliament from Quebec were openly anti-Semitic during that period. [3]

In 1999 David Damien organized a gathering in Winnipeg of two thousand Christians from across Canada. They met to confess the sins of our forebears. Damien describes the event: 'Churches across the nation came together in one accord, not to hear a speaker, but to travail and lament and weep and humble themselves and decide to turn back from their wicked ways and seek God's forgiveness and the healing of our nation.'[4] They came especially to repent of Christian mistreatment of Jews through the centuries. As part of a covenant established with the Jewish people, 'A seven-point statement endorses Israel, repents for Christian persecution of Jews, and denounces "the unbiblical beliefs of the church that have resulted in attitudes and actions that have produced harm to the Jews".'[5]

The concern to work for reconciliation, expressed by Pohl and Damien, is to be highly commended. From Northern Ireland to the Middle East, bitterness continues to inflame relations between peoples. Seeking to effect reconciliation between races, as much as between individuals, is a Christian duty.

EXPLANATION

Practical problems and unanswerable questions, however, besiege attempts to confess ancestral sin. If I am to confess the sins of my ancestors, how can I discover them all? Am I only to confess the sins that have marred group relationships, such as the treatment of aboriginals by settlers? What about more personal sins? For example, how my grandfather might have treated his neighbour? Do these sins of long ago still haunt us? If so, does that not make past sin more powerful than present grace?

How far back should I go? As an Anglo-Saxon Canadian should I confess the sins of my English forebears against the Irish, against Scottish tenant farmers, against the indigenous peoples of India, Pakistan, Kenya or South Africa? Should I go back and confess the sins committed by the crusaders against the Turks?

If I have a mixture of Irish/Scots/English/French ancestry, how do I untangle my responsibilities? Do I avail myself of Mormon genealogical studies? Even when I discover the wrongs, how do I find the correct forum in which to express my confession?

I don't believe God expects me to engage in this kind of historical dig. I have enough personal sins to confess without embarking on such an odyssey. While well meaning, this pursuit is based upon a misunderstanding of Scripture.

At first glance the practice appears to have biblical support. In the second commandment we read that the Lord is 'a jealous God, punishing the children for the sin of the fathers to the third and fourth generation of those who hate me' (Exodus 20:5; Deuteronomy 5:9). This maxim, reiterated in Leviticus, Numbers, Isaiah and Jeremiah, seems to prove that ancestral guilt clings to descendants.

While the prophets reiterated this principle, they actually corrected its misinterpretation. Ezekiel uses most of chapter 18 to assert that personal responsibility, not ancestral guilt, is fundamental. He denounces what had become a proverb in Israel: 'The fathers have eaten sour grapes, and the children's teeth are set on edge' (Jeremiah 31:29; Ezekiel 18:2). He points out that 'The soul who sins is the one who will die. The son will not share the guilt of the father, nor will the father share the guilt of the son' (Ezekiel 18:20).

Each of us is responsible for our own sins, not the sins of others. Parental guilt does not cling to children. Justice abhors this idea.

What then is meant by those verses in the law that describe God punishing the children for their father's sins? Ezekiel again gives us the clue. He explains that a child is free of parental guilt, 'who sees all the sins his father commits, and though he sees them, he does not do such things' (18:14). In other words, guilt is not passed down from generation to generation automatically, but through the free choice of each generation.

As children grow they mimic what they see in their homes. They are trained to react a certain way, to value certain things and to view life in a certain way. Unless they deliberately choose to reject what is wrong, they naturally adopt the way their family exhibits acceptance or prejudice towards other groups. Family upbringing powerfully influences their views of integrity or dishonesty, hard work or laziness, truthfulness or falsehood, sexual purity or impurity. Peer groups outside the home add their powerful influences.

TO SUMMARIZE

TO SUMMARIZE

The Scriptures do not substantiate the belief that we need to confess the sins of our ancestors in order to take away hindrances to revival.

Unresolvable problems cluster around any attempt to confess the sins of those who have gone before us. Some verses apparently teach that guilt is passed on to succeeding generations (Exodus 20:5; Deuteronomy 5:9). However, the prophets — notably Ezekiel — correct the misinterpretation of these texts. Ezekiel affirms that 'the soul who sins is the one who will die. The son will not share the guilt of the father, nor will the father share the guilt of the son' (18:20).

The only sense in which guilt is passed on from generation to generation occurs when descendants deliberately, or unconsciously, adopt the sinful patterns of their forbears. Ezekiel explains that a child is free of parental guilt who 'sees all the sins his father commits, and … does not do such things' (18:14).

If children act like their ancestors, they incur the same guilt as their ancestors, not because they carry on their shoulders their ancestors' guilt, but because they have personally perpetuated their fathers' sins. Without deliberate rejection of a family's — or a society's — warped values, a child innately carries on that family's traditions. And in this way, ancestral sin is visited on children through many generations.

An Italian may inherit the vendetta of a forebear. An Afghan may grow up sworn to avenge his grandfather. A Hutu may hate a Tutsi, and vice versa. A child from an aristocratic home may grow up looking down on commoners. Children brought up among Irish Orangemen throw stones at Irish Catholics who respond in kind.

Unfortunately, racial profiling still exists — even prospers. Sadly, many Arabs, Sikhs and Hindus living in western democracies became targets of a backlash of anger following the attack on the U.S. on September 11, 2001. Such an unjust response must be personally greeted with revulsion — and annihilated. Ironically, a much more virulent racial profiling was being practised by the terrorists who labelled America as the Great Satan and felt justified in killing any American, innocent or otherwise.

Every Arab is not a terrorist, neither is every American anti-Islamic — few are. It makes as much sense to lay guilt on every Arab or Irish nationalist or Afghan or white person as it does to lay guilt on this generation for the deeds of the previous one. This generation is not personally responsible for how our ancestors treated people generations ago. I can no more receive forgiveness for my father's sins, than I can repent for him.

What then can we do about the strained relationships caused by our fathers and their ancestors? We cannot change the past. We can, with God's help, change the present. How? Let me make five suggestions.

Firstly, *we should reject racial profiling.* We must stop holding the innocent progeny of certain races or societal groups responsible for the sins of their parents. To halt this injustice, we must examine our lifestyles and repudiate any attitude or pattern of behaviour towards others that reflects bitterness, prejudice or anger. How do we feel towards people of other ethnic groups? Uncomfortable? Superior? Frustrated? What if they have done grievous violence to our race?

In 1985 when President Reagan of the United States laid a wreath on the graves at Bitburg in Germany, some felt this was too soon after the war. It became an international incident reviving the hates and fears of Hitler's world — in particular, the horror that was the Holocaust. Jewish demands for justice had not been fully met. Admittedly, those of us who did not go through that ghastly time can do little but shut our mouths in silence. We have little right to offer Jewish survivors advice.

If we continue, however, to nurture bitterness towards new generations of Germans, or Serbs, or Irish or Palestinians or Jews, where will it all end but in everlasting conflict? At the time Reagan made this gesture, Kenneth Kantzer wrote an editorial in *Christianity Today*. 'The President's motive was clear: he wished to make a powerful affirmation of good will towards the German people, and to toughen the bonds of mutual respect and co-operation already existing between the nations... President Reagan was affirming to the German nation our forgiveness of its wrong against the American people by its involvement in the Nazi war crimes and in the death camps of Europe. He could do this only because he is the president of all American Jews, and because those terrible crimes in the final analysis were against us all, and not against the Jews only. When Chancellor Helmut Kohl responded for West Germany, the two leaders together affirmed reconciliation of the two nations.'[6]

Secondly, *we must make it known that we repudiate many of the ways, for example, our forebears treated the aboriginal peoples*, our Anglo-Saxon ancestors treated the French of Quebec or the English treated those in their colonies, although much good was also accomplished! While I do not believe we can confess the sins of our ancestors, we can apologize for their mistakes. There is power in apology.

I want to distinguish here between confession of sin, which of necessity involves personal guilt, and apology, which does not. As noted in chapter seven, apology is appropriate where others are harmed due to our human fallibility — perhaps an accident or an oversight. While

ILLUSTRATION

we are not personally responsible for being born into a certain race or family, there is a real link with our forbears. This link ought to produce within us a certain remorse for the harmful actions of those who preceded us. This remorse can be expressed by an open apology.

In November 2000, Baptist pastor Doug Blair joined a group of Christians in Ottawa. They had gathered to apologize to survivors of the ill-fated World War 2 refugee ship *St Louis*. Blair's great uncle was the director of the Canadian immigration branch that refused entry to the *St Louis* and its 900 Jewish refugees in 1939. Twenty-five ageing survivors had joined them. 'In introducing himself to the survivors, Blair said it was presumptuous of him to address them as friends. With his son, Joel, standing with him on the podium, Blair apologized. "That which was done to you was so wrong. To the extent that my family was a part of that, I'm sorry," he said. After they stepped down, they were surrounded by people who embraced them. And one of the survivor leaders said: "Let me be the first to call you 'friend.'"'[7]

For years the Worldwide Church of God led people astray with their own cultic brand of legalism. Several years ago, in an amazing movement of the Spirit, that church returned to the historic Christian faith. In the March/April 1996 issue of the *Plain Truth* magazine, Joseph Tkach Jr, pastor general, published an apology on behalf of the entire church. He confessed that they had pursued a works-righteousness that obscured the riches of grace to be found in Jesus Christ and led them to become self-righteous and judgemental. He wrote in part: 'We have been wrong… We make no attempt to cover up the doctrinal and scriptural errors of our past… We stand today at the foot of the cross — the ultimate symbol of all reconciliation… We desire to meet there with anyone we may have injured… So to all members, former members, co-workers and others — all who have been casualties of our past sins and mistakes of doctrine, I extend my sincerest heartfelt apologies.'[8]

Thirdly, *we must try to develop harmonious relationships* with those nearby who represent aggrieved groups. In distant places around the globe sincere Christians attempt to mediate peace in the midst of conflict.

Pakistan, like other countries, is rife with territorial and ethnic tensions. Most Panjabi Christians feel threatened by the Muslim majority. Love for lost Muslims has been rare among professing Christians. New believers from the downtrodden Marvari tribe feel the sting not only of Muslim disdain but also of Panjabi Christian prejudice. During the sixteen years we ministered there, we frequently had to reiterate God's hatred of ethnic pride. We were often involved in bringing Panjabi and Marvari believers together. Others in our mission had to attempt resolution of disputes with cruel Panjabi landlords who used these land-less sharecroppers abominably.

THINK ABOUT IT

Neve Shalom/Wahat al-Salam (Oasis of Peace) is a village half way between Jerusalem and Tel Aviv. Ever since it was founded in 1972 it has been a remarkable experiment in peaceful co-existence. Christian, Jewish and Muslim children learn together in both Hebrew and Arabic.

Undated devotional in *Daily Bread*, Grand Rapids: Radio Bible Class.

Conscious of our fractured world and how little forgiveness is injected into conflict, 'Former President Jimmy Carter, Archbishop Desmond Tutu and former missionary Elisabeth Elliot are leading a $10 million "Campaign for Forgiveness Research".'[9]

In Muslim Bangladesh, converts to Christ can face hatred and real danger. How they act can often defuse conflict. A young believer was eating his rice one evening in a Bangladeshi village when he heard an uproar. His uncle and some of his friends were about to kill a teenage thief who had taken refuge in their village with $4000 he had stolen from the shop where he worked. Leaving his rice, the believer went to reason with the angry crowd. He pleaded for the life of the thief and the return of the money. Eventually he was successful in leading them towards mercy and restitution.

When he returned the money to the shopkeeper he was offered $200 for himself. This he refused, but he did plead for the boy-thief to be forgiven and restored to his job. As a result of this episode, the young believer gained a lot of respect in his village. Shortly afterwards he was asked to mediate in a dispute between two quarrelling village groups.[10]

Fourthly, *we should model racial harmony in our churches*. One way to do this is to encourage the development of churches in which people from many backgrounds worship together. My understanding of God's ideal is a church in which people from diverse social strata and cultures worship together in harmony. Paul reminds the Gentiles that formerly they were 'foreigners to the covenants of the promise ... but now in Christ Jesus you who once were far away have been brought near through the blood of Christ. For he himself is our peace, who has made the two one and has destroyed the barrier, the dividing wall of hostility' between Jew and Gentile (Ephesians 2:12-14). 'There is neither Jew nor Greek, slave nor free, male nor female, for you are all one in Christ Jesus' (Galatians 3:28).

One of the greatest delights of my pastorate in a Toronto church was to see a congregation develop from many ethnic backgrounds: English, Irish and Scots; Europeans from various countries; Jamaicans, Spanish, Sri Lankans, Indians, Filipinos and Chinese. A foretaste of heaven!

Fifthly, *we should work hard to right the wrongs perpetrated by our ancestors*. Christians ought to be involved in a multiplicity of efforts to demonstrate the love of Christ to alienated groups: Australian aboriginals; North American First Nations; Arabs stigmatized by terrorists; or the people of Northern Ireland.

In Canada this means that the denominations that ran boarding schools in which indigenous children were abused must attempt to redress these wrongs. Rev. John Congram, moderator of the Presbyterian Church in Canada, feels that Christian forgiveness can be far too glib. 'There is no real forgiveness unless you are prepared to face the pain of what happened.' For his church, this meant confessing the wrongs they had committed against Indian people in residential schools and through their past policies as well as taking concrete steps to redress wrongs. Several other Canadian denominations are involved in seeking to right past policies that wrested children from their parents and robbed them of their cultural identity. (I would prefer to use the word 'apology' rather than 'confession'.)

We must face the pain caused by past actions and do what we can to heal the resultant hurts. Seeking to mediate peace where there is bitterness and conflict is a fundamentally Christian task. 'Blessed are the peacemakers.' Realistically, however, we cannot expect overwhelming success in this venture. As long as sin reigns in human hearts, conflicts will continue to erupt. Jesus predicted that 'wars and rumours of wars' would increase until the end of time. While the vast majority of human conflict, as explained by James, arises from competition with others over what humans lust after, some conflict does arise from gospel proclamation.[11]

Presentation of the gospel of peace — which is our first duty — creates conflict. The gospel that calls people to repent of their sins, to acknowledge Christ before men, to take up his cross daily and to follow him, presents them with a stark choice. Accepting this invitation immediately alienates those who bow to Christ as Lord from those who do not. This is why Jesus warned: 'I have come to turn "a man against his father, a daughter against her mother, a daughter-in-law against her mother-in-law — a man's enemies will be the members of his own household"' (Matthew 10:35-36). Jesus explained: 'Do not suppose that I have come to bring peace to the earth. I did not come to bring peace, but a sword' (10:34).

Ultimate success in all efforts to mediate peace is not promised. Nevertheless, there is a clear role for Christian peacemakers. The place to start is among those nearest us, especially those who have been harmed by our own ancestors. We cannot ask forgiveness for their sins but we can express revulsion at their actions and offer heart-felt apologies on their behalf.

QUESTIONS FOR DISCUSSION

1. *Read Ezekiel 18. Summarize, in your own words, the teaching of the chapter under the following headings:*
   a. *The parable quoted by the people of his day.*
   b. *Why they quoted the parable.*

DISCUSS IT

c. Example one, verses 5-9.
d. Example two, verses 10-13.
e. Example three, verses 14-18.
f. Example four, verses 25-29.
g. Briefly summarize God's justice and mercy as seen here, especially from verses 19-24.

2. *Consider your own family, community and nation, and answer the one question below that seems most important in your situation.*
   a. *List groups that are most commonly caricatured or racially profiled in your community.*
   b. *What is there about earlier generations of your own race or family that you find repugnant?*
   c. *What groups in your community are currently suffering from discrimination?*
   d. *What groups in your community are currently suffering as a result of evils committed against them by earlier generations?*
   e. *How does your local church feel about having various ethnic groups participating in worship and leadership?*

3. *List any ways that Christians in your nation are working to right wrongs committed by earlier generations.*

4. *Prayerfully select one way you will personally work to alleviate past wrongs; e. g. apologize to someone for past wrongs, encourage or befriend a racially targeted person, support a ministry working with a group unjustly treated by your forebears, etc.*

CHAPTER FIFTEEN

HOW CAN I BECOME A FORGIVING PERSON?

LOOK IT UP

BIBLE REFERENCE

'Blessed are the peacemakers, for they will be called sons of God' (Matthew 5:9).

INTRODUCTION

If love makes the world go round, forgiveness is the oil that lubricates the gears. We know that becoming a forgiving person is the will of God. We have no problem with the theory. We may have even been able to apply the principles in the past. We've asked for forgiveness from those we have hurt. We've given forgiveness to those who have grieved us. By the help of the Spirit, we've been able to forget past incidents that caused us resentment. Life is good. The sun is shining brightly. Then out of the blue someone comes along who treats us abysmally. Before we know it the old anger is aroused and resentment is unravelling the very relationship that we worked so hard to establish.

Strength to face unexpected conflicts comes with Christian maturity. Maturity includes the ability to deal with conflict in a merciful and forgiving way. That maturity is developed within us by the Holy Spirit. The Spirit prepares us for temptations and trials by opening up the Scriptures to our understanding, helping us relate to the trials and triumphs of biblical characters and drawing us closer and closer to Jesus Christ. Through it all he toughens our resistance to evil.

We do not have to wait to be mature in Christ, however, to forgive! Every Christian, at whatever stage he or she might be in, is called upon to forgive. Indeed part of the maturing process is learning to forgive. Our growth in grace is stunted when we fail to forgive. Jesus Christ understands that some of us have a harder time dealing with forgiveness than others. He knows the culture and family atmosphere in which we were saved. What he looks for is our longing to please him; our desire to become more forgiving. He treasures every attempt, no matter how feeble. Remember, he is gentle and tender in heart. 'A bruised reed he will not break, and a smouldering wick he will not snuff out' (Matthew 12:20). Nevertheless, no matter how many times we stumble, we must each time re-commit ourselves to become more mature in our response to those who provoke us.

THINK ABOUT IT

A forgiving person is one who, out of a profound sense of being personally forgiven a great debt by God, is quick to ask forgiveness from another; who repudiates anger, bitterness and a desire for revenge to initiate a loving approach to whoever may have hurt him or her; and who offers to freely forgive and forget the injury caused, with the hope that reconciliation may be achieved.

EXPLANATION

Developing Christian maturity can be viewed from various biblical perspectives. It is putting on 'the full armour of God, so that when the day of evil comes, you may be able to stand your ground' (Ephesians 6:13). It is showing our love in what we do. 'Let us not love with words or tongue but with actions and in truth' (1 John 3:18). Maturity is a fruit of the Spirit. 'But the fruit of the Spirit is love, joy, peace, patience, kindness, goodness, faithfulness, gentleness and self-control' (Galatians 5:22-23). This fruit is nurtured as we 'live by the Spirit ... keep in step with the Spirit' through crucifying 'the sinful nature with its passions and desires' (5:24-25).

Another perspective on maturity is found in the Sermon on the Mount. Here we find Christ proclaiming the charter of the kingdom. In this amazing sermon he describes the principles that should govern those who bow to him as king. The Beatitudes, in particular, are indispensable (see Matthew 5:3-12). They comprise eight foundational attitudes we should have towards God, towards ourselves and towards others. As their title — Beatitudes — implies, they are sensibilities of the heart and mind. The person whose heart beats in rhythm with this metronome will act in a gracious, forgiving way towards others. And that person will be truly happy, i.e. blessed.

Let me change the simile. Like Joseph's coat of many colours, we can compare the Beatitudes to a garment of eight layers. This suit of attitudes is specifically designed to protect us from the chilling blast of charge and counter-charge that freezes relationships. Christ Jesus, himself, created this ensemble to insulate us from the cold anger, icy resentment and bitter retaliation that arms the cycle of alienation. Clothed in the Beatitudes we will be able to respond warmly to others — even to those who slander us. We will become forgiving people.

Let us beseech Jesus Christ our Lord to clothe us with these eight attitudes:

- Poverty of spirit — true humility;
- Mourning — anguish over sin;
- Meekness — freedom from self-concern;
- Hunger for righteousness — longing for holiness;
- Mercy — pity for those in misery;
- Purity of heart — single-minded focus on the glory of God;
- Peace — commitment to resolve conflicts;
- Persecution — acceptance of inevitable persecution.

Trying to face conflict or offence without having adopted these attitudes would be like trying to brave an arctic storm in shorts and a T-shirt.

No one, that I know, has written or preached more expressively on this portion of Matthew's Gospel than Dr Martyn Lloyd-Jones. His *Studies in the Sermon on the Mount* is a rich and uplifting exposition.[1] It is deeply satisfying because it brings together many strands and weaves them into a gospel cord that binds us to Christ.

EXPLANATION

I urge you to make every effort to get a copy of this commentary. Read it; underline it; pray your way through it. You will not be the same.

Without careful attention to the biblical text, however, Lloyd-Jones' insights will be lost to us. I would suggest, therefore, that you open your Bible at Matthew 5 as we consider how these attitudes reflect those of forgiving people. After each, I will suggest a prayer we could pray that encapsulates that Beatitude.

1. Blessed are the poor in spirit. Our Lord is not talking here about the kind of poverty of spirit exemplified in those who are shallow, thoughtless or dull. Nor does he describe weakness or lack of courage. Humility is in view. Not the humility of one who is modest about his status, education or talents. It is the humility of one who realizes that he is spiritually bankrupt, sinful, fallen — depraved in thought, word and deed. Those who are poor in spirit cry out as the tax collector did in the temple, 'God, have mercy on me, a sinner' (Luke 18:13). This first quality concerns what we looked at in chapter 2, the importance of having a proper view of ourselves — particularly our own depravity.

In chapter 5 we considered the story of Sydna Massé, whose next-door neighbour was killed by a jealous lover. Hatred and bitterness consumed her until involvement in a Bible study led her to recognize her own sinfulness in the sight of God.

In her case, as in ours, recognizing a poverty of spirit precedes a display of biblical forgiveness.

PRAYER: Lord, help me to recognize the extent to which depravity has corrupted my mind, heart and will without letting me become given over to despair. Use this self-knowledge to stifle pride and give me understanding and empathy towards others.

2. Blessed are those who mourn. A view of the malignant nature of iniquity leads to mourning for sin. When we realize that sin is a slap in the face of the gracious God, in whom we live and from whom we derive every good and perfect gift, we begin to mourn. Another term for this anguish is conviction of sin. This kind of conviction is first of all introspective. But it also includes anguish for the sins of the world. We mourn the degrading influence of sin on the gentle world that God has created.

Paradoxically, conviction leads to comfort. How? We discover personal comfort in the person of Christ who died to atone for our sins. We also find comfort in knowing that there will come a time when sin is destroyed, when Satan is cast into the lake of fire, when there will be a new heaven and a new earth. Discovering that holiness, not iniquity, will write the final chapter of earth's history, gives us immeasurable comfort.

PRAYER: *Lord, deliver me from a flippant, indifferent attitude towards my own sin and the sins of the world. Help me to find abiding comfort in the cross of Christ and abounding hope in the knowledge that history is moving towards a time when sin will be banished.*

3. Blessed are the meek. A certain meekness results from mourning over our own poverty of spirit. We recognize that at the root of our rebellion against God and our conflict with others is our own self-centredness. Aghast at the selfishness that moves us to interpret everything in terms of our own comfort and happiness, we begin to become concerned about others. We haltingly begin to seek the pleasure of God. This new sensitivity to our own egocentrism makes us think twice before asserting ourselves to acquire what we want.

Lloyd-Jones points out that meekness is neither indolence, flabbiness, niceness nor weakness of personality. It is not being defensive, sorry for oneself or overly sensitive. Instead of retaliating for offences, the meek person develops the spiritual strength to persevere graciously. This patience leads to inheriting the earth. In God's economy it is not competition, aggression or advertising that wins the day. Like Abraham in dealing with Lot, Moses in leading the people of Israel and David with Saul, the meek possess a spiritual strength that brings them through victoriously.[2]

Meekness is a crucial quality among those who forgive. In his excellent commentary on

Matthew, William Hendriksen comments: 'It describes the person who is not resentful. He bears no grudge. Far from mulling over injuries received, he finds refuge in the Lord and commits his way entirely to him ... the willingness rather to suffer than to inflict injury. The meek person leaves everything in the hand of him who loves and cares.'[3]

THINK ABOUT IT

> 'The man who is meek ... is free from self in its every shape and form — self-concern, pride, boasting, self-protection, sensitiveness, always imagining people are against him, a desire to protect self and glorify self. That is what leads to quarrels between individuals, that is what leads to quarrels between nations; self-assertion.'
>
> Lloyd-Jones, *Sermon on the Mount*, p. 79.

PRAYER: *Gentle Jesus, King of Kings, deliver me from this preoccupation with myself, my plans, my desires, my concerns. Deliver me from self-assertion and self-protection. Help me to develop the spiritual strength that is meekness while I trust in you to fulfil your purposes.*

4. Blessed are those who hunger and thirst for righteousness. Lamentation over our own sins and the sins of the world creates within us a longing for what is missing. We hunger and thirst for righteousness. We yearn

EXPLANATION

for the will of God to be done on earth as it is in heaven. We thirst for goodness, mercy, kindness, unselfishness, thankfulness, worship and respect.

A supernatural meekness, produced by the Holy Spirit, has led us to recognize that these qualities cannot be acquired by aggressive effort or imposed on other people. Our longing leads us to prayer. In prayer we are surprised by joy! How? The Spirit applies the blood of Christ to our convicted hearts. We discover that we have been freely justified — declared righteous for the sake of Christ in whom we believe. The exhilarating sense of being justified thrills us to the core. As day follows day we also long for practical holiness of life. The Holy Spirit satisfies this desire by, imperceptibly, transforming us into the image of Christ. When we look within we realize that we have such a long, long way to go to become Christ-like. And yet when we look back over a year, ten years, we marvel at what God has done. The Holy Spirit has been progressively sanctifying us. Truly, we 'are being transformed into his likeness with ever-increasing glory, which comes from the Lord, who is the Spirit' (2 Corinthians 3:18).

PRAYER: *Heavenly Father, my attempts to be good, even godly, fail to fill the hunger of my heart. Fill me instead with the joy that comes from knowing that the righteousness I can never earn has been given to me freely through your Son, our Lord Jesus. Thrill me again with your justifying grace. And out of that joy create a deeper, and more practical thirst for practical godliness. Help me to do what is good, right and loving today.*

5. *Blessed are the merciful.* Once we have tasted the mercy of God it is unthinkable that we would not become merciful towards others. We feel pity for those in misery. We discover a desire to relieve their suffering.

Some have interpreted this Beatitude to mean that we must first show mercy to others before God will show mercy to us. However, if this were the case, none of us would ever taste mercy from God. His mercy and grace must transform us before we can be anything but vindictive, indifferent and selfish. In other words, if we interpret this passage in a legal manner it would mean that we are saved by works — our work of forgiving others. As Lloyd-Jones points out, this would negate the whole of the New Testament teaching on grace found in verses such as 'While we were still sinners, Christ died for us' (Romans 5:8).

Lloyd-Jones goes on to explain this Beatitude, and the parallel passage in the Lord's Prayer, as follows: 'Our Lord is really saying that I am only truly forgiven when I am truly repentant. To be truly repentant means that I realize I deserve nothing but punishment, and that if I am forgiven it is to be attributed entirely to the love of God and to His mercy and grace, and to nothing else at all. But I go further; it means this. If I am truly repentant and realize my position before God, and realize that I am only forgiven in that way, then of necessity I shall forgive those who trespass against me.'[4]

While mercy is not natural to us, when we yield to Christ we begin to develop the supernatural tendency to feel pity even for those who vilify us. Mercy led Sydna to write a letter to her friend's killer. Mercy led Colleene Hackett to forgive her neighbour. Mercy, through a renewed commitment to Christ, led Mark Thistle to forgive his attacker. Mercy led Jeff Schulte to feel pity for his father.

PRAYER: *Merciful Father, deliver me from concentrating on how I am feeling. Help me to feel pity and empathy even for those who hurt me. Cleanse my heart of anger and bitterness.*

6. Blessed are the pure in heart. We who gaze into the depths of our own poverty-stricken hearts mourn the defilement we see there. We long to replace with purity the cloying selfishness that waylays us at every turn. This desire reshapes our vision of what is important in life.

Jesus is not teaching here that once we are redeemed, we become absolutely pure in heart. The term 'pure in heart' relates to what he says later in this sermon. The citizen of the kingdom is not to spend his energies laying up treasure on earth but rather treasure in heaven (see Matthew 6:19-21). This new motivation unifies his fragmented desires so that he can concentrate on seeking holiness. 'If therefore thine eye be single, thy whole body will be full of light' (Matthew 6:22, AV). Pureness of heart, in this sense, means purity of motivation, freedom from hypocrisy, sincerity. In Psalm 86 David prays: 'Give me an undivided heart, that I may fear your name' (v. 11).

Singleness of vision enables us to see God in the events of life. We do not feel we are at the mercy of chaotic, unpredictable forces. We know that the Lord sovereignly rules the universe. 'In all things God works for the good of those who love him, who have been called according to his purpose' (Romans 8:28). Such a vision helps us to trust God even when attacked or vilified by another. Our heart is purified from unworthy anger and bitterness because our vision of the greatness and glory of God enables us to see that there are much greater issues at stake than our own ego.

PRAYER: *Lord Jesus, my heart is far from pure. It is besmirched by selfishness that moves me to be always concerned about my own desires and how to fulfil them, my own ego and how to enhance it. Clarify my vision so that my heart is focused on you, your kingdom, your glory.*

7. Blessed are the peacemakers. Purity of vision moves us to actively endeavour to bring peace where there is conflict. Having become poor in spirit through a glimpse of our own hearts, we can see clearly that the cause of all conflict is sin — both ours and that of others. Lloyd-Jones writes: 'The explanation of all our troubles is human lust, greed, selfishness, self-centredness; it is the cause of all the trouble and the discord, whether between individuals, or between groups within a nation, or between nations themselves ... [the cause] is not political, it is not economic, it is not social. The answer once more is essentially and primarily theological and doctrinal.'[5]

Our growing vision of the kingdom enables us to see that the main antidote to conflict is the gospel of peace. Because of this reality, missions — proclaiming the gospel to the ends of the earth — become high on our priority. To use the psalmist's terminology, we see the nations rage against God and each other and our hearts bleed for this affront to the glory of God (see Psalm 2). Locally, we take the initiative in asking for forgiveness if we have caused offence. Where we have been the one sinned against, we graciously seek reconciliation with those who have hurt us.

As peacemakers, we are not appeasers or busybodies but we do actively seek peace wherever we live and serve. Our longing is that the glory and harmony resident in the triune God may be demonstrated on earth.

PRAYER: *Prince of peace, deliver me from causing unrighteous conflict. Help me to seek reconciliation with any who are alienated from my fellowship. Give me the courage and the wisdom to become involved in promoting harmony first in the church and then in my community.*

8. Blessed are those who are persecuted because of righteousness. We might naturally assume that our attempts to bring peace and manifest humility, mercy and integrity would be respected. The Scriptures, however, prepare us to expect the opposite. We may face rejection that could degenerate into outright persecution.

Lloyd-Jones points out that the rejection followers of Christ may experience is not because they act in an objectionable way or are foolish, busybodies or over-zealous.[6] Citizens of the kingdom are persecuted 'because of righteousness'. The way genuine disciples act is an affront to the lifestyle of others. It makes them feel uncomfortable or guilty. The peacemaker may even find both parties to a dispute turning against him.

Jesus' warning is clear: 'If they persecuted me, they will persecute you also… They will treat you this way because of my name' (John 15:20-21). Throughout history this has been the case. Before Christ, the prophets were persecuted. After Christ, early Christians endured unimaginable persecution. In the twentieth century there have been more Christian martyrs than at any time in history.

The disciple who adopts the Beatitudes as his own should not expect an easier time in the world. Jesus explains that his followers can expect insults, false accusations and all kinds of evil to be done to them (Matthew 5:11-12).

EXPLANATION

This reality should at least prepare us for the inevitable. Let's not be surprised by controversy, conflict, resentment, slander — whatever might come our way. We live in a fallen world. We can prepare ourselves, however, by beseeching the Holy Spirit to develop within us the Beatitudes.

PRAYER: *Lord, keep me from bringing shame on your name by acting foolishly but also help me not to take rejection personally when I am doing your will. Give me the courage to own your name even where it will arouse antagonism. Help me not to be surprised when serving you brings opposition.*

Eight revolutionary attitudes! As we become more humble and more serious about sin, meeker and hungrier for holiness, more merciful and more focused, we will become more forgiving people. We will be peacemakers. Although conflicts and hurts may rain down upon us, peace and harmony will flourish where our lives touch others.

THINK ABOUT IT

'Life without forgiveness is hell on earth. And the reason is abundantly clear. Life without forgiveness is really life without God. The motivation for Christ's coming to earth and

> the purpose of the cross is centred on God's concern for forgiveness... The consequences that flow out of forgiveness remind us that God's ways are good ways. Forgiveness restores relationships, heals inner spirits, releases resentment and subdues hate. Forgiveness turns off the mental video tape of feeling hurt and calculating how to get even.'
>
> Don Posterski, 'Forgive or else', *Christian Week*, 1 April 1997, p. 7

Making the Beatitudes our attitudes will prepare us to endure conflicts victoriously; conflicts that might tempt us to anger, hatred, resentment or retaliation. We will become forgiving people: people who, out of a profound sense of being personally forgiven a great debt by God, are quick to forgive others; who repudiate anger, bitterness and a desire for revenge to initiate a loving approach to whoever may have hurt us; who offer to freely forgive and forget the injury caused, with the hope that reconciliation may be achieved.

Forgiveness is revolutionary! It is also one of the most beautiful words in the Bible. Let's embrace it today!

QUESTIONS FOR DISCUSSION

1. *We can view developing Christian maturity from various perspectives. For example, according to 2 Peter 3, it is growing 'in the grace and in the knowledge of our*

Lord and Saviour Jesus Christ'. How is Christian development (sanctification) described in the following verses?

a. Galatians 5:22-23
b. Galatians 5:24-25
c. Ephesians 6:13
d. 1 John 3:19

2. *Read Matthew 5:1-12. Pick two or three of the Beatitudes that are most important at this stage in your life. Use the references below to further describe, in your own words, what each teaches.*

   a. Poverty of spirit (Philippians 2:3; Numbers 12:3; Matthew 23:12)
   b. Mourning (Psalm 51:1-10)
   c. Meekness (Matthew 5:38-42; Luke 9:23)
   d. Hunger for righteousness (Colossians 3:1-14)
   e. Mercy (Micah 6:8; Matthew 25:31-46)
   f. Purity of heart (Matthew 6:33; Romans 12:1-2; Philippians 3:7-11)
   g. Peacemaking (Romans 12:18; Hebrews 12:14; James 3:17-18)
   h. Persecution (1 Peter 4:12-19)

3. *Write out a prayer, in your own words, for each of the Beatitudes that you chose in question two. Then pray to God for the help of his Spirit in each of these areas.*

THE GUIDE

NOTES

NOTES

Chapter 1

1. Philip Yancey, *What's So Amazing About Grace?* Grand Rapids: Zondervan, 1997.
2. Quoted in Yancey, *What's So Amazing?*
3. CBS Evening News, 15 April 1998.
4. Insert in a column by Haroon Siddiqui, *The Toronto Star*: 12 December 1999, p.A15.
5. Story in *Daily Bread*, 10 March (uncertain year, pre-1984), Grand Rapids: Radio Bible Class.
6. *Ibid*.

Chapter 2

1. Larry Crabb, *The Real Problem*, Chapter 5, 'Bring Home the Joy', Grand Rapids: Zondervan, 1998, p.81.
2. From the hymn 'Come Thou Fount of every blessing', by Robert Robinson (1735-90).
3. Crabb, *The Real Problem*, p.85.
4. David Augsburger, *The Freedom of Forgiveness*, Moody, 1988, p.33.

Chapter 3

1. J. I. Packer, *Hot Tub Religion*, Wheaton: Tyndale, 1987, p.9.
2. *Westminster Shorter Catechism*.
3. James Orr, General Editor, *Forgiveness*, ISBE, Grand Rapids: Eerdmans, 1955, p.343.

Chapter 4

1. Quoted in Gary Thomas, *The Forgiveness Factor*, paper posted on web, Christianity Today.com, 02/10/2001 (www.christianitytoday.com/ct/2000/001/1.38.html) pp.2-3.
2. Ann Landers, 'It's better to forgive', Toronto: *Sunday Star*, 29 January 1984, p.D4.
3. *Ibid.*
4. Jean Walcott Wilson, *Parenting Prodigals*, Focus on the Family, Nov. 2000, p.14.
5. Quoted in Yancey, *What's So Amazing?* p.83.
6. Neil T. Anderson, *The Bondage Breaker*, Eugene, Oregon: Harvest House, 1993, p.195.
7. 'Hope for a nation', *SIMNow*, Winter 1999, p.6.

Chapter 5

1. Yancey, *What's So Amazing?* pp.85-6.
2. Larry Crabb, *Inside Out*, Colorado Springs, Colorado: NavPress, 1988, p.133.
3. Yancey, *What's So Amazing?* p.97.
4. Augsburger, *Freedom of Forgiveness*, pp.16-7.
5. Lewis Smedes, *Forgive and Forget*, New York: Simon & Schuster (Penguin), 1984.
6. Colleene J. Hackett, *Focus on the Family newsletter*, April 1995, p.1.
7. Quoted by Gary Thomas, *Forgiveness Factor*, p.18.
8. *Ibid.*, p.3.
9. Sydna Massé, *Forgiveness: Breaking the Chains*, Focus on the Family, January 1999, p.13.
10. *Ibid.*

Chapter 6

1. David Seamands, 'Perfectionism: Fraught with Fruits of Self-Destruction', *Christianity Today*, 10 April 1981, pp.24-5 (quoted by Yancey).
2. Dr James Dobson's *Focus on the Family Bulletin*, December 1996.
3. Verdell Goulding summarizing Robert Enright in 'The Psychology of Forgiveness', *The People's Magazine*, Winter 2001, p.4.
4. Smedes, as quoted by Gary Thomas, *Forgiveness Factor,* p.14.
5. Robert D. Enright as quoted by Gary Thomas, *Forgiveness Factor,* p.20.
6. Gary Thomas, *Forgiveness Factor,* p.8.
7. *Freed From Bitterness*, undated bulletin from Partners International.
8. *Ibid.*
9. *Ibid.*

Chapter 7

1. Matthew Henry, *Commentary on the Whole Bible, Volume 6*, Revell, p.764.
2. Marshall Shelley, *Well-Intentioned Dragons*, Leadership/Word, 1985, p.21.
3. Editorial, 'Driving is all the rage', *The Northumberland News*, 14 August 2001, p.5.
4. *Ibid.*
5. Gerald L. Sittser, *A Grace Disguised — How the Soul Grows Through Loss*, Grand Rapids: Zondervan, 1996, pp.119, 126.

6. *Ibid.*, p.127.
7. Smedes, as quoted by Gary Thomas, *Forgiveness Factor*, p.13.
8. Augsburger, *Freedom of Forgiveness*, p.46.
9. W. E. Vine, *An Expository Dictionary of New Testament Words*, Lynchburg: The Old-Time Gospel Hour edition, undated, p.453.
10. *Ibid.*, p.452.
11. Quoted by Thomas, *Forgiveness Factor*, p.13.
12. Augsburger, *Freedom of Forgiveness,* p.28.
13. Massé, *Forgiveness*, p.13.
14. Robert D. Enright and Joanna North, editors, *Exploring Forgiveness*, University of Wisconsin Press, 1998 (quoted by Gary Thomas, *Forgiveness Factor,* p.19).

Chapter 8

1. Jules Ostrander, 'God Comes to Nebraska Panhandle', Regina: *Revival Fellowship News*, Fall, 1990, p.2.
2. Ruth Veltkamp, 'A Lesson in Forgiveness from a Fulani Christian', *Missionary Monthly*, June-July, 1986, p.26.
3. Bob Welch, *Restoration*, Focus on the Family, June 1998, p.7.
4. *Ibid.*
5. *Ibid.*
6. Suggested books include: David Augsburger, *When Caring Is Not Enough — Resolving Conflicts Through Fair Fighting,* Scotsdale: Herald, 1983; G. Douglass Lewis, *Resolving Church Conflicts — A Case Study Approach for Local Congregations*, New York: Harper & Row, 1981; Charles J. Keating, *Dealing With Difficult People — How*

You Can Come Out On Top In Personality Conflicts, New York: Paulist Press, 1984; Robert D. Dale, *Surviving Difficult Church Members*, Nashville: Abingdon Press, 1984.
7. Augsburger, *Freedom of Forgiveness,* p.28.
8. A prayer letter sent by Rick Oickle, January 1997.
9. Yancey, *What's So Amazing?* p.115.
10. Thomas, *Forgiveness Factor,* p.18.
11. Yancey, *What's So Amazing?* p.116.
12. Leslie K. Tarr, 'Faith brings reconciliation in prisons of Northern Ireland', *Toronto Star*, 13 August 1983, p.H8.
13. Yancey, *What's So Amazing?* p.135.
14. *Writer's Digest* newsletter, David E. Meadows, 18 Sept. 2001, http://newsletters.fwpublications.com.

Chapter 9

1. Laura J. Yoder Jones, 'Forgiveness — based on a true story', *TeenPower*, May 1987.
2. Eddie Askew, *No Strange Land*, Brentford, Middlesex: 1987, p.81. ©The Leprosy Mission International, 80 Windmill Road TW8 0QA.
3. Summary by Augsburger of William Barclay, *The Daily Study Bible,* Edinburgh: St Andrew, 1962, pp.266-8.
4. Beverly Bush Smith, *When to Zip Your Lip*, Wheaton: Power for Living, 1985 (012085), p.5.
5. Augsburger, *Freedom of Forgiveness*, pp.33-4.

6. Quoted by Steve Brown in 'Steve's Letter', *Keylife newsletter*, July 1998.

Chapter 10

1. Timothy Ernst, 'Restorative Grace — An interview with Gordon MacDonald', *Faith Today*, September/October 1988, pp.38-9.
2. Ron Lee Davis, *A Forgiving God in an Unforgiving World*, Eugene, Oregon: Harvest House, 1984, p.62.
3. *Westminster Confession*, chapter XXX, part IV.
4. Shepherd of Hermas, A.D. c.150, quoted by Marshall Shelley, *Leadership* editorial, Spring 1988, p.3.
5. *Ibid.*
6. *Ibid.*

Chapter 11

1. Philip Foster, letter, *Evangelical Times*, Aug. 1999, p.22.
2. Christopher Rogers, letter, *Evangelical Times*, Nov. 1999, p.17.
3. Those who emphasis man's free will rather than God's sovereign will.
4. Davis, *Forgiving God*, p.99.
5. John Peter Lange, Gen. Ed. *Commentary on the Holy Scriptures — Luke*, Grand Rapids: Zondervan, 1969, p.259.
6. Matthew Henry, *Matthew Henry's Commentary*, Revell, reprint from 1721, Volume V, p.765.
7. 'Victim forgives his attacker', *Jubilee*, Dec./Jan. 1989, p.1.

8. *Ibid.*
9. Steve Brown, *The Radical Nature of Grace,* Maitland, Florida, series, undated.

Chapter 12

1. Beulah Petersen, 'Restitution', *Decision*: July-August 1984, p.16.
2. Undated handout circulated by Ralph Sutera, a Canadian preacher on revival.
3. *Ibid.*
4. Bob Harvey, 'Christians and Crime', *Faith Today*, Sept./Oct. 2000, p.30.
5. By this reference I do not mean to condone everything in the Christian Restorative Justice movement. Some in the movement deny original sin, reject punitive justice and uphold theologically liberal — and thus heretical —ideas.
6. *Daily Bread*, undated.
7. Bob Harvey, *Faith Today*, p.31.
8. *Ibid.*, p.33.
9. Peter Hum and Joanne Laucius, 'Forgiveness sets family killer free', *Toronto Star*, 20 June 1999, A3.
10. Yancey, *What's So Amazing?* p.127.
11. *Ibid.*, p.125.

Chapter 13

1. Ray Felten, 'Past Sins Forgiven', *Advice for Today,* Grand Rapids: Spectrum, p.56.
2. Martin Luther, 'Lectures on Galatians 1535,

Chapters 1-4', *Luther's Works*, Volume 26, Saint Louis: Concordia, 1963, p.26.

3. *Ibid.*, p.5.
4. *Daily Bread*, undated.
5. R. David Roberts, 'Forgiveness', Wheaton, *Leadership*, 1987, p.48. (Roberts quotes from an article in *Guideposts*.)
6. Charles Bracelen Flood, 'Lee, The Last Years', cited by Michael Williams in *Leadership*, Fall 1984, p.47.

Chapter 14

1. A tenant farmer who gives a share of his crop as rent.
2. Rudy & Marny Pohl, *A Matter of the Heart: Healing Canada's Wounds*, Belleville, ON: Essence Publishing, 1998.
3. Laureen Moe, 'Anti-Semitic history hinders Canada's spiritual destiny', *Christian Week*, 9 June 1998, p.3.
4. Doug Koop, 'Four covenants and a prayer call', *Christian Week*, 3 Aug. 1999, p.1.
5. *Ibid.*
6. Kenneth S. Kantzer, 'Bitburg: Must We Forgive?', *Christianity Today*, 12 July 1985.
7. Lloyd Mackey, 'Pastor renounces ancestors' decision', *Christian Week*, 28 November 2000, p.5.
8. Joseph Tkach, Jr, 'Forgive Us Our Trespasses', reprinted in *Christianity Today*, 15 July 1996; p.30 from the March/ April issue of the *Plain Truth* magazine.
9. Gary Thomas, *Forgiveness Factor*, p.1.
10. Paul Harland, Prayer letter, March 1987.
11. See James 4:1-3 as explained in chapter 5.

NOTES

Chapter 15

1. Dr Martyn Lloyd-Jones, *Studies in the Sermon on the Mount, Volume One,* Grand Rapids: Eerdmans, reprint, 1961.
2. *Ibid.*, pp.66-70.
3. William Hendriksen, *New Testament Commentary — Exposition of the Gospel According to Matthew*, Grand Rapids, Baker, 1973, p.272.
4. Lloyd-Jones, *Sermon on the Mount,* p.102.
5. *Ibid.*, p.119.
6. *Ibid.*, pp.130-1.

BIBLIOGRAPHY

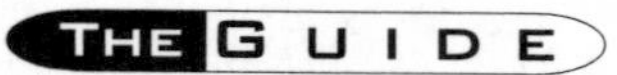

BIBLIOGRAPHY

Books, Forgiveness

Augsburger, David. *The Freedom Of Forgiveness*, Moody, 1988.

Davis, Ron Lee. *A Forgiving God*, Eugene, Oregon: Harvest House, 1984.

Enright, Robert D. and North Joanna, editors. *Exploring Forgiveness*, University of Wisconsin Press, 1998.

Pohl, Rudy & Marny. *A Matter of the Heart: Healing Canada's Wounds*, Belleville, ON: Essence Publishing, 1998.

Sittser, Gerald L. *A Grace Disguised — How the Soul Grows Through Loss*, Grand Rapids: Zondervan, 1996.

Smedes, Lewis. *Forgive and Forget*, New York: Simon & Schuster (Penguin), 1984.

Thomas, Gary. *The Forgiveness Factor*, paper posted on web: Christianity Today.com, 02/10/2001 (www.christianitytoday.com/ct/2000/001/1.38.html) pp.2-3.

Books, General

Anderson, Neil T. *The Bondage Breaker*, Eugene, Oregon: Harvest House, 1993.

Askew, Eddie. *No Strange Land*, Brentford, Middlesex: The Leprosy Mission International, 1987.

Augsburger, David. *When Caring Is Not Enough — Resolving Conflicts Through Fair Fighting*, Scotsdale: Herald, 1983.

Crabb, Larry. *Inside Out*, Colorado Springs, Colorado: NavPress, 1988.

Crabb, Larry. *The Real Problem*, Grand Rapids: Zondervan, 1998.

Dale, Robert D. *Surviving Difficult Church Members*, Nashville: Abingdon Press, 1984.

Keating, Charles J. *Dealing With Difficult People — How You Can Come Out On Top In Personality Conflicts*, New York: Paulist Press, 1984.

Lewis, G. Douglas. *Resolving Church Conflicts — A Case Study Approach for Local Congregations*, New York: Harper & Row, 1981.

Packer, J. I. *Hot Tub Religion*, Wheaton: Tyndale, 1987.

Yancey, Philip. *What's So Amazing About Grace?*, Grand Rapids: Zondervan, 1997.

Bible Study Sources

Hendriksen, William. *New Testament Commentary – Exposition of the Gospel According to Matthew*, Grand Rapids: Baker, 1973.

Henry, Matthew. *Commentary on the Whole Bible, Volumes 5 and 6*, Revell, reprint from 1721.

Lange, John Peter, General Editor. *Commentary on the Holy Scriptures — Luke*, J. J. Van Oosterzee, Grand Rapids: Zondervan, 1969.

Lloyd-Jones, Dr D. Martyn. *Studies in the Sermon on the Mount,* Volume One, Grand Rapids: Eerdmans, reprint, 1961.

Luther, Martin. 'Lectures on Galatians 1535', Chapters 1-4, *Luther's Works*, Volume 26, Saint Louis: Concordia, 1963.

Orr, James, General Editor. *Forgiveness*, ISBE, Grand Rapids: Eerdmans, 1955.

Vine, W. E. *An Expository Dictionary of New Testament Words*, Lynchburg: The Old-Time Gospel Hour edition, undated.

Articles

Augsburger, David. Summary of William Barclay, *The Daily Study Bible*, Edinburgh: St Andrew, 1962.

Brown, Steve. *Keylife* newsletter, 'Steve's Letter', July 1998.

Brown, Steve. *The Radical Nature of Grace*, Maitland, Florida, series, undated.

Daily Bread. Grand Rapids: Radio Bible Class, undated.

Editorial, 'Driving is all the rage'. *The Northumberland News*, 14 August 2001.

Ernst, Timothy. 'Restorative Grace — An interview with Gordon MacDonald', *Faith Today*, September/October 1988.

Felten, Ray. 'Past Sins Forgiven', Grand Rapids: Spectrum, *Advice for Today*, undated.

Flood, Charles Bracelen. 'Lee, The Last Years', cited by Michael Williams in *Leadership*, Fall 1984.

Goulding, Verdell. Summary of Robert Enright in 'The Psychology of Forgiveness', *The People's Magazine*, Winter 2001.

Hackett. Colleene J. *Focus on the Family newsletter*, April 1995.

Harvey, Bob. 'Christians and Crime', *Faith Today*, Sept/Oct. 2000.

Hum, Peter and Laucius, Joanne. 'Forgiveness sets family, killer free', *Toronto Star*, 20 June 1999.

Jones, Laura J. Yoder. 'Forgiveness — based on a true story', *TeenPower*, May 1987.

Kantzer, Kenneth S. 'Bitburg: Must We Forgive?', *Christianity Today*, 12 July 1985.

Koop, Doug. 'Four covenants and a prayer call', *Christian Week*, 3 Aug. 1999.

Landers, Ann. 'It's better to forgive', Toronto: *Sunday Star*, 29 January 1984.

Mackey, Lloyd. 'Pastor renounces ancestor's decision', *Christian Week*, 28 Nov. 2000.

Massé, Sydna. *Forgiveness: Breaking the Chains*, Focus on the Family, January 1999.

Moe, Laureen. 'Anti-Semitic history hinders Canada's spiritual destiny', *Christian Week*, 9 June 1998.

Ostrander, Jules. 'God Comes to Nebraska Panhandle', Regina: *Revival Fellowship News*, Fall 1990.

Petersen, Beulah. 'Restitution', *Decision*: July-Aug. 1984.

Roberts, R. David. 'Forgiveness', Wheaton, *Leadership*, 1987.

Seamands, David. 'Perfectionism: Fraught with Fruits of Self-Destruction', *Christianity Today*, 10 April 1981.

BIBLIOGRAPHY

Shelley, Marshall. *Well-Intentioned Dragons*, Leadership/Word, 1985.

Shepherd of Hermas. A.D. c.150 , quoted by Marshall Shelley, *Leadership* editorial, Spring 1988.

Smith, Beverly Bush. *When to Zip Your Lip*, Wheaton: Power for Living, 1985 (012085).

Tarr, Leslie K. 'Faith brings reconciliation in prisons of Northern Ireland', *Toronto Star*, 13 Aug. 1983.

Tkach, Joseph Jr. 'Forgive Us Our Trespasses', reprinted in *Christianity Today*, 15 July 1996, from the March/April issue of the *Plain Truth* magazine.

Veltkamp, Ruth. 'A Lesson in Forgiveness from a Fulani Christian', *Missionary Monthly*, June-July 1986.

'Victim forgives his attacker'. *Jubilee*, Dec./Jan. 1989.

Welch, Bob. *Restoration*, Focus on the Family, June 1998.

Wilson, Jean Walcott. *Parenting Prodigals*, Focus on the Family, Nov. 2000.

Writer's Digest newsletter. David E. Meadows, 18 Sept. 2001: http://newsletters.fwpublications.com.

THE GUIDE

TOPICAL INDEX

TOPICAL INDEX

THE GUIDE

SELECTED SCRIPTURE INDEX

SELECTED SCRIPTURE INDEX